Practical Ideas
That Really Work
for Students with
Autism Spectrum Disorders

Practical Ideas
That Really Work
for Students with
Autism Spectrum Disorders

Kathleen McConnell

Gail Ryser

pro·ed
An International Publisher

8700 Shoal Creek Boulevard
Austin, Texas 78757-6897
800/897-3202   Fax 800/397-7633
Order online at http://www.proedinc.com

© 2000 by PRO-ED, Inc.
8700 Shoal Creek Boulevard
Austin, Texas 78757-6897
800/897-3202   Fax 800/397-7633
Order online at http://www.proedinc.com

Printed in the United States of America

5   6   7   8   9   10   04

Contents

Introduction

We created *Practical Ideas That Really Work for Students with Autism Spectrum Disorders* for educators who work with students who have autism or other developmental disorders that interfere with their ability to learn and to function in social situations. The materials are intended for use with students in grades preschool through 12 and include two main components:

- *An evaluation form with a rating scale and idea matrix.* The rating scale portion of the evaluation form is a criterion-referenced measure for evaluating behaviors that impact student learning and social interactions. The items on the scale are specific descriptors that are correlated to the DSM–IV indicators for autistic disorder. All DSM–IV criteria for autistic disorder and Asperger's disorder are included on the scale. Additionally, many of the items apply to childhood disintegrative disorder and Rett's disorder. On the third page of the evaluation form we have included a table that indicates which items relate to each of the four disorders. Because many of the criteria for childhood disintegrative disorder and Rett's disorder are biological in nature, items for these criteria are not included on the rating scale. The ideas matrix on the last page of the evaluation form provides a systematic way of linking the results of the rating scale to interventions. We hope that educators use the matrix as a tool for selecting effective interventions to meet each student's specific needs.

- *A book of practical ideas.* The ideas were written to assist teachers and other professionals in improving students' social interactions and communication skills and in decreasing their repetitive and stereotypical patterns of behaviors. The ideas were developed to meet the needs of students with a range of pervasive developmental disorders. The name of the book reflects our understanding that students with these disorders can exhibit a wide spectrum of skills and behaviors related to social interactions, communication, and repetitive/stereotypical behaviors. The book contains an explanation of each idea, along with reproducible worksheets, examples, illustrations, and tips designed for easy implementation.

There are also many references to other materials that teachers may find useful.

The next section of this introduction will describe the development of the rating scale and the ideas, and then provide directions for their use.

The Rating Scale

The criterion-referenced rating scale is intended for use by teachers or other professionals to rate children and adolescents according to the DSM–IV criteria for autistic disorder, Asperger's disorder, childhood disintegrative disorder, and Rett's disorder. The measure was designed to assist teachers in conducting a careful and thorough assessment of the specific problems to guide the selection of intervention strategies. This scale is not intended to be used to diagnose these disorders, rather it is intended as a tool for determining intervention strategies and writing IEP goals and objectives.

The rating scale is divided into the three areas of autistic disorder defined by the DSM–IV: Social Interactions, Communication, and Repetitive/Stereotyped Patterns of Behavior. The measure consists of 39 items; three items for each of the 12 DSM–IV criteria and three for receptive language. Professionals are to answer the following question when rating a student: To what degree do the behaviors listed interfere with the student's ability to function in the learning or social environments? Next, professionals use the 4-point Likert scale to complete a rating, with a 0 meaning not at all like the student, almost never interferes and a 3 meaning exactly like the student, almost always interferes. For each criterion, the range of possible scores is 0 to 9; the higher the score, the more the behavior interferes with the student's ability to function in the learning and social environments.

The criterion-referenced measure was field-tested in three school districts in Texas with 50 students identified as having autism. The students ranged in age from 3 to 18 years of age with 12 females and 38 males. An item analysis was conducted using this sample and the resulting reliability coefficients were .91 for social interactions,

.90 for communication, and .92 for repetitive/stereotyped behaviors. The magnitude of these coefficients strongly suggests that the rating scale possesses little test error and that users can have confidence in its results.

Practical Ideas That Really Work

Teachers and other educators are busy people with many responsibilities. In our discussions with teachers, supervisors, and counselors about the development of this product, they consistently emphasized the need for materials that are practical, easy to implement in the classroom, and not overly time consuming. We appreciated their input and worked hard to meet their criteria as we developed the ideas in this book. In addition, we conducted an extensive review of the literature, so that we stayed focused on ideas supported by data documenting their effectiveness. The result is a book with 37 ideas, many with reproducible masters, and all grounded in research and the collective experience of the two of us, as well as the many educators who advised us and shared information with us.

Assessment often provides much useful information to educators about the strengths and deficits of students. However, unless the information gathered during the assessment process impacts instruction, its usefulness for campus-based educators is limited. We designed the idea matrix so that educators can make the direct link between the information provided by the rating scale and instruction in the classroom. We think that this format stays true to our purpose of presenting information that is practical and useful.

Directions for Using the Materials

The professional (a special education teacher, general education teacher, counselor, or other educator with knowledge of the student) should begin by completing the Evaluation Form for the child who has been identified as autistic or with another pervasive developmental disorder. In addition, the professional can use this product with children who exhibit problems functioning in the learning or social environment because of poor social interactions or communication skills, or who exhibit repetitive or stereotypical patterns of behavior.

As an example, Torrance's completed Evaluation Form is provided in Figure 1 on page 5. Space is provided on the front of the form for pertinent information about the student being rated, including name, birth date, age, school, grade, and educational setting. In addition, the name of the rater, the dates the student is observed, and the amount of time the rater spends with the student can be recorded here. Also included on the front of the form are the DSM–IV criteria for autistic disorder.

Pages 2 and 3 of the Autistic Spectrum Disorders Evaluation Form contain the rating scale. The items are divided into the three sections defined by the DSM–IV criteria for autistic disorder: Social Interactions, Communication, and Repetitive/Stereotypical Patterns of Behavior. This section provides the instructions for administering and scoring the items. Space is also provided to total the items for each DSM–IV criterion, to check the three problems to target for immediate intervention, and to record the intervention idea and its starting date. At the bottom of the rating scale is a table that depicts which items of the rating scale are aligned to the DSM–IV criteria for four disorders: autistic disorder, Asperger's disorder, childhood disintegrative disorder, and Rett's disorder.

The last page of the Evaluation Form contains the Ideas Matrix. After choosing the three priority problems to target for immediate intervention, the professional should turn to the Ideas Matrix and select an intervention that corresponds to that problem. The professional should write the idea number and the starting date in the space provided on the rating scale.

For example, Torrance received the highest ratings in two areas of Communication (Conversation [9] and Make-Believe Play [7]) and one area of Social Interactions (Sharing Enjoyment and Interests [6]). His teacher has targeted these three areas and has chosen Ideas 37, 1, and 9 from the Ideas Matrix. Because the area of major concern is conversation, the teacher will begin with Idea 37 on September 6.

After selecting one or more ideas from the matrix, the teacher can read the explanation, then go ahead and implement the first idea. To aid in implementation, most of the 37 ideas have at least one reproducible form on the page(s) immediately following the explanation. A small light-bulb icon in the top right-hand corner of the idea page indicates an accompanying form. Some ideas did not lend themselves to a reproducible form, but are supported with explanations, suggestions for use, illustrations, tips, resource lists, and boxes of further information. Ideally, the teacher or other professional should evaluate the effectiveness of each intervention. In our example with Torrance, this could be accomplished by recording the number of skills he has mastered in the area of communication as it pertains to conversation during a 6- to 8-week period. The teacher can either move on to the second problem at this point or work on more than one problem simultaneously. In the case of Torrance, the teacher plans to use Idea 1, Puppet Play, with Torrance to improve both his conversational skills and his ability to engage in make-believe play.

Supporting Evidence for the Practical Ideas

The next section provides references for journal articles, books, and monographs that contain supporting data for the practical ideas in the book. These references provided us with rationales and supporting research for specific methodologies and should assist interested professionals who are interested in more detailed information. We have grouped the references by general category, according to our focus during our research.

Improving Receptive and Expressive Communication

Durand, M. (1990). Severe behavior problems: A functional communication training approach. In R. Horner, G. Dunlap, & R. Koegel (Eds.), *Generalization and maintenance: Life-style changes in applied settings* (pp. 221–241). Baltimore: Brookes.

Hart, B., & Rogers-Warren, A. K. (1978). A milieu approach to teaching language. In R. L. Schiefelbusch (Ed.), *Language intervention strategies* (pp. 193–235). Baltimore: University Park Press.

Manning, A., & Katz, K. (1991). Facilitating functional communication with echolalic language users. *Focus on Autistic Behavior, 6*(3), 1–7.

Watson, L. R., Lord, C., Schaffer, B., & Schopler, E. (1989). *Teaching spontaneous communication to autistic and developmentally handicapped children.* Austin, TX: PRO-ED.

Cueing and Prompting Students

Alberto, P.A., Sharpton, W. R., Briggs, A., & Stright, M. G. (1986). Facilitating task acquisition through the use of a self-operated auditory prompting system. *Journal of the Association for Persons with Severe Handicaps, 11,* 85–91.

Maurice, C. (Ed.), Green, G. G., & Luce, S. C. (Co-Eds.). (1996). *Behavioral intervention for young children with autism: A manual for parents and professionals* (pp. 188–189). Austin, TX: PRO-ED.

Stahmer, A.C., & Schreibman, L. (1992). Teaching children with autism appropriate play in unsupervised environments using a self-management treatment package. *Journal of Applied Behavior Analysis, 25*(2), 447–459.

Taber, T. A., Seltzer, A., Heflin, L. J., & Alberto, P. A. (1999). Use of self-operated auditory prompts to decrease off-task behavior for a student with autism and moderate mental retardation. *Focus on Autism and Other Developmental Disabilities, 14*(3), 159–166.

Wolery, M., Ault, M. J., & Doyle, P. M. (1992). *Teaching students with moderate to severe disabilities.* New York: Longman.

Using Functional Behavioral Analysis

Calloway, C. J., & Simpson, R. L. (1998). Decisions regarding functions of behavior: Scientific versus informal analysis. *Focus on Autism and Other Developmental Disabilities, 13*(3), 167–175.

Cipani, E. (1998). Three behavioral functions of classroom noncompliance: Diagnostic and treatment implications. *Focus on Autism and Other Developmental Disabilities, 13*(2), 66–72.

Teaching Students Through Imitation

Lovaas, O. I. (1987). Behavioral treatment and normal educational and intellectual functioning in young autistic children. *Journal of Consulting and Clinical Psychology, 55,* 3–9.

Maurice, C. (Ed.), Green, G. G., & Luce, S. C. (Co-Eds.). (1996). *Behavioral intervention for young children with autism: A manual for parents and professionals* (pp. 187–188). Austin, TX: PRO-ED.

Olgetree, B. T. (1995). Movement as a strategy to encourage pre-language communication. *Focus on Autistic Behavior, 9*(6), 12–14.

Schopler, E., Mesibov, G. B., & Hearsy, K. (1995). Structured teaching in the TEACCH system. In E. Schopler & G.B. Mesibov (Eds.), *Learning and cognition in autism* (pp. 243–268). New York: Plenum.

Using Positive Reinforcement

Dyler, K. (1987). The competition of autistic stereotyped behavior with usual and specially assessed reinforcers. *Research in Developmental Disabilities, 8,* 606–626.

Stahmer, A.C. (1995). Teaching symbolic play skills to children with autism using pivotal response training. *Journal of Autism and Developmental Disorders, 25*(2), 123–141.

Williams, T. I. (1993). Brief report: Vocabulary development in an autistic boy. *Journal of Autism and Developmental Disorders, 23* (1), 185–191.

Wolery, M., Ault, M. J., & Doyle, P. M. (1992). *Teaching students with moderate to severe disabilities.* New York: Longman.

Developing and Implementing Social Skills Programs

Norris, C., & Dattilo, J. (1999). Evaluating effects of a social story intervention on a young girl with autism. *Focus on Autism and Other Developmental Disabilities, 14*(3), 180–186.

Simpson, R., Myles, B. S., Sasso, G. M., & Kemps, D. (1997). *Social skills for students with autism.* Reston, VA: Council for Exceptional Children.

Strain, P.S. (1983). Generalization of autistic children's social behavior change: Effects of developmentally integrated and segregated settings. *Analysis and Intervention in Developmental Disorders, 3,* 23–34.

Swaggart, B. L., Gagnon, E., Bock, S. J, Earles, T. L., Quinn, C., Myles, B. S., & Simpson, R. L. (1995). Using social stories to teach social and behavioral skills to children with autism. *Focus on Autistic Behavior, 10*(1), 1–16.

Structuring the Environment To Promote Learning

Maurice, C. (Ed.), Green, G. G., & Luce, S. C. (Co-Eds.). (1996). *Behavioral Intervention for Young Children with Autism: A manual for parents and professionals* (pp. 185–186). Austin, TX: PRO-ED.

Simpson, R. L., & Zionts, P. (2000). *Autism: Information and resources for professionals and parents* (2nd ed.) (pp. 94–95). Austin, TX: PRO-ED.

Designing and Using Visual Strategies

Bondy, A., & Frost, L. (1994). The picture exchange communication system. *Focus on Autistic Behavior, 9*(3), 1–17.

Grandin, T. (1995). *Thinking in pictures.* New York: Doubleday.

Quill, K. A. (1995). Visually cued instruction for children with autism and pervasive developmental disorders. *Focus on Autistic Behavior, 10*(3), 10–20.

Quill, K. A. (1997). Instructional considerations for young children with autism: The rationale for visually cued instruction. *Journal of Autism and Other Developmental Disorders, 27,* 697–714.

Practical Ideas That Really Work

for Students with Autism Spectrum Disorders

Kathleen McConnell
Gail Ryser

Evaluation Form

Name __Torrance Wilson__

Birth Date __4-12-91__   Age __9__

School __Carver Elementary__   Grade __3__

Rater __Ms. Martins (teacher)__

Educational Setting __self-contained classroom__

Dates Student Observed: From __8-15-00__ To __9-4-00__

Amount of Time Spent with Student:

Per Day __4 hrs.__   Per Week __20 hrs.__

DSM-IV Diagnostic Criteria for Autistic Disorder

A. A total of six (or more) items from (1), (2), and (3), with at least two from (1), and one each from (2) and (3):

(1) qualitative impairment in social interaction, as manifested by at least two of the following:

  (a) marked impairment in the use of multiple nonverbal behaviors such as eye-to-eye gaze, facial expression, body postures, and gestures to regulate social interaction

  (b) failure to develop peer relationships appropriate to developmental level

  (c) a lack of spontaneous seeking to share enjoyment, interests, or achievements with other people (e.g., by a lack of showing, bringing, or pointing out objects of interest)

  (d) lack of social or emotional reciprocity

(2) qualitative impairments in communication as manifested by at least one of the following:

  (a) delay in, or total lack of, the development of spoken language (not accompanied by an attempt to compensate through alternative modes of communication such as gesture or mime)

  (b) in individuals with adequate speech, marked impairment in the ability to initiate or sustain a conversation with others

  (c) stereotyped and repetitive use of language or idiosyncratic language

  (d) lack of varied, spontaneous make-believe play or social imitative play appropriate to developmental level

(3) restricted repetitive and stereotyped patterns of behavior, interests, and activities, as manifested by at least one of the following:

  (a) encompassing preoccupation with one or more stereotyped and restricted patterns of interest that is abnormal either in intensity or focus

  (b) apparently inflexible adherence to specific, nonfunctional routines or rituals

  (c) stereotyped and repetitive motor mannerisms (e.g., hand or finger flapping or twisting, or complex whole-body movements)

  (d) persistent preoccupation with parts of objects

B. Delays or abnormal functioning in at least one of the following areas, with onset prior to age 3 years: (1) social interaction, (2) language as used in social communication, or (3) symbolic or imaginative play.

C. The disturbance is not better accounted for by Rett's Disorder or Childhood Disintegrative Disorder.

Note. From the *Diagnostic and Statistical Manual of Mental Disorders, Fourth Edition*, 1994, Washington, DC: American Psychiatric Association. Copyright 1994 by American Psychiatric Association. Reprinted with permission.

Additional copies of this form (#9342) may be purchased from PRO-ED, 8700 Shoal Creek Blvd., Austin, TX 78757-6897 800/897-3202, Fax 800/397-7633

(continues)

Figure 1. Sample Evaluation Form, filled out for Torrance.

Rating Scale

DIRECTIONS

❶ In your opinion, to what degree do the behaviors listed interfere with the student's ability to function in the learning or social environments? Use the following scale to circle the appropriate number:

0 = Not at all like the student, almost never interferes.
1 = Somewhat like the student, sometimes interferes.
2 = Very much like the student, frequently interferes.
3 = Exactly like the student, almost always interferes.

❷ Total the ratings and record in the Total box.

❸ Put a check in the Immediate Intervention column by the top three problems. (Give special consideration to those items with totals ≥ 6.)

❹ Select up to three ideas from the matrix for each problem, and write the number and start date for each in the blanks provided in the last column.

BEHAVIOR	RATING (Not at all / Somewhat / Very much / Exactly)	TOTAL	IMMEDIATE INTERVENTION	IDEAS; START DATE

Social Interactions

Nonverbal Behaviors
1 Avoids making eye contact or appears to be looking through other people. — 0 ①　2　3
2 Does not communicate emotions or interest through facial expressions. — 0　1　②　3 — [4] — ○ — ___ ___
3 Reacts negatively to physical contact (e.g., acts fearful or is totally passive). — 0 ①　2　3

Peer Relationships
1 Does not react to the presence of peers. — 0 ①　2　3
2 Does not initiate relationships with peers. — 0　1 ②　3 — [5] — ○ — ___ ___
3 Does not build or maintain friendships. — 0　1 ②　3

Sharing Enjoyment and Interests
1 Does not show accomplishments to others. — 0　1　2 ③
2 Shows little interest in everyday events. — 0 ①　2　3 — [6] — ✓ — 9 ___
3 Does not share enjoyment about an object or activity. — 0　1 ②　3

Social Reciprocity
1 Does not kiss, hug, or shake hands with others. — 0　1 ②　3
2 Does not take turns when playing simple games with others. — 0 ①　2　3 — [5] — ○ — ___ ___
3 Prefers to be alone. — 0　1 ②　3

Communication

Expressive Language
1 Does not speak spontaneously to others. — 0 ①　2　3
2 Does not use gestures or signs to communicate with others. — 0 ①　2　3 — [4] — ○ — ___ ___
3 Does not let others know through words or gestures his or her needs or desires. — 0　1 ②　3

Conversation (Only rate if student has spoken language.)
1 Does not initiate conversations with others. — 0　1　2 ③ — — — 37　9-6-00
2 Fails to use greetings (e.g., "hello") or courteous phrases (e.g., "please," "thank you"). — 0　1　2 ③ — [9] — ✓ — 1 ___
3 Does not ask others questions. — 0　1　2 ③

Stereotyped Language (Only rate if student has spoken language.)
1 Echolalic (i.e., repeats what he or she hears, rather than responding appropriately). — 0 ①　2　3
2 Perseverates (i.e., repeats the same phrase over and over). — 0 ①　2　3 — [4] — ○ — ___ ___
3 Recites common phrases heard on television or radio. — 0　1 ②　3

(continues)

Figure 1. Continued.

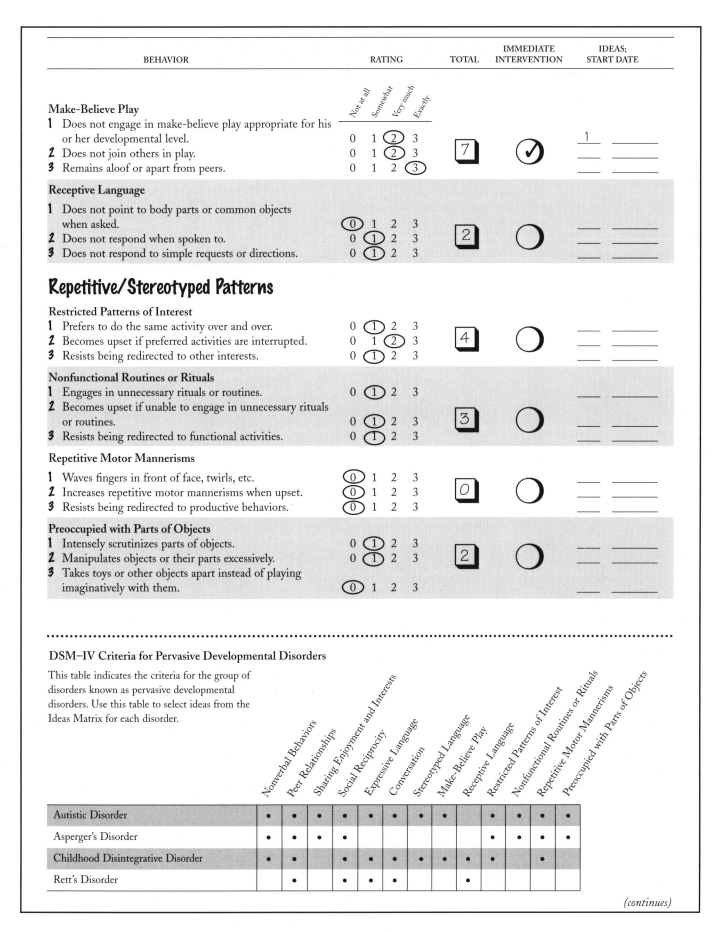

BEHAVIOR	RATING				TOTAL	IMMEDIATE INTERVENTION	IDEAS; START DATE
	Not at all	Somewhat	Very much	Exactly			

Make-Believe Play
1 Does not engage in make-believe play appropriate for his or her developmental level. — 0 1 (2) 3
2 Does not join others in play. — 0 1 (2) 3
3 Remains aloof or apart from peers. — 0 1 2 (3)
TOTAL: [7] — Immediate Intervention: (✓) — Ideas: 1

Receptive Language
1 Does not point to body parts or common objects when asked. — (0) 1 2 3
2 Does not respond when spoken to. — 0 (1) 2 3
3 Does not respond to simple requests or directions. — 0 (1) 2 3
TOTAL: [2] — Immediate Intervention: ( )

Repetitive/Stereotyped Patterns

Restricted Patterns of Interest
1 Prefers to do the same activity over and over. — 0 (1) 2 3
2 Becomes upset if preferred activities are interrupted. — 0 1 (2) 3
3 Resists being redirected to other interests. — 0 (1) 2 3
TOTAL: [4]

Nonfunctional Routines or Rituals
1 Engages in unnecessary rituals or routines. — 0 (1) 2 3
2 Becomes upset if unable to engage in unnecessary rituals or routines. — 0 (1) 2 3
3 Resists being redirected to functional activities. — 0 (1) 2 3
TOTAL: [3]

Repetitive Motor Mannerisms
1 Waves fingers in front of face, twirls, etc. — (0) 1 2 3
2 Increases repetitive motor mannerisms when upset. — (0) 1 2 3
3 Resists being redirected to productive behaviors. — (0) 1 2 3
TOTAL: [0]

Preoccupied with Parts of Objects
1 Intensely scrutinizes parts of objects. — 0 (1) 2 3
2 Manipulates objects or their parts excessively. — 0 (1) 2 3
3 Takes toys or other objects apart instead of playing imaginatively with them. — (0) 1 2 3
TOTAL: [2]

DSM–IV Criteria for Pervasive Developmental Disorders

This table indicates the criteria for the group of disorders known as pervasive developmental disorders. Use this table to select ideas from the Ideas Matrix for each disorder.

	Nonverbal Behaviors	Peer Relationships	Sharing Enjoyment and Interests	Social Reciprocity	Expressive Language	Conversation	Stereotyped Language	Make-Believe Play	Receptive Language	Restricted Patterns of Interest	Nonfunctional Routines or Rituals	Repetitive Motor Mannerisms	Preoccupied with Parts of Objects
Autistic Disorder	•	•	•	•	•	•	•	•		•	•	•	•
Asperger's Disorder	•	•	•	•						•	•	•	•
Childhood Disintegrative Disorder	•	•		•	•	•	•	•	•	•		•	
Rett's Disorder		•		•	•	•		•					

(continues)

Figure 1. Continued.

Ideas Matrix

Ideas	Social Interactions				Communication					Repetitive Patterns			
	Nonverbal Behaviors	Peer Relationships	Sharing Enjoyment and Interests	Social Reciprocity	Expressive Language	Conversation	Stereotyped Language	Make-Believe Play	Receptive Language	Restricted Patterns of Interest	Nonfunctional Routines or Rituals	Repetitive Motor Mannerisms	Preoccupied with Parts of Objects
1 Puppet Play	●	●	●	●	●	⊙	●	⊙	●	●		●	
2 What To Teach Next	●	●	●	●	●	●	●	●	●	●	●	●	●
3 Direct Teach Social Skills	●	●	●	●	●	●	●	●	●	●	●	●	●
4 Write Your Own	●	●	●	●	●	●	●	●	●	●	●	●	●
5 Read the Sign	●	●	●	●	●	●	●	●	●	●	●	●	●
6 Your Turn/My Turn	●	●	●	●	●	●	●	●	●				
7 Nice Looking	●			●		●							
8 Learn To Imitate	●	●	●	●	●	●	●	●	●				
9 Get Excited	●	●	⊙	●	●	●	●		●				
10 Follow the Music	●	●	●	●				●	●	●	●	●	●
11 Step-By-Step	●	●	●	●				●					
12 Talk Prompters	●	●	●	●	●	●	●	●	●	●			
13 Get Predictable	●	●	●	●	●	●	●	●	●				
14 Take One and Pass It On	●	●	●	●	●	●	●	●	●				●
15 Conversation Cards		●	●	●	●	●	●	●	●				
16 Bring Out the Noise		●	●	●	●	●	●		●				
17 Talk Back Cards		●	●	●	●	●	●						
18 Choice Cards			●		●				●	●	●		
19 The Daily Scoop			●	●		●			●	●	●		
20 Yes/No Cards						●	●	●	●				
21 "I" Cue Card						●	●	●					
22 Subtle Sabotage						●	●		●				
23 Teacher Prompts						●	●	●	●				
24 Great Games						●	●	●	●				
25 Count Down							●			●	●	●	●
26 Follow and Find										●	●	●	
27 Now–Next Picture Map										●	●	●	
28 Schedule It										●	●	●	
29 Touch, Show, or Find									●				
30 Say or Tell Me					●				●				
31 Do This Instead of That										●	●	●	●
32 Activity Notebook										●	●	●	●
33 Less Time → Choice Time										●	●	●	●
34 Nickels, Dimes, or Quarters	●	●	●	●	●	●	●	●	●	●	●	●	●
35 Card Counters	●	●	●	●	●	●	●	●	●	●	●	●	●
36 Use What Works	●	●	●	●	●	●	●	●	●	●	●	●	●
37 Watch and Learn	●	●	●	●	●	⊙	●	●	●	●	●	●	●

Figure 1. Continued.

Idea 1
Puppet Play

The DSM–IV definition of autism includes a description related to play. Students with autism or a related disorder often fail to play with others (social play) and usually do not engage in make-believe play. One way to encourage play, especially make-believe, is to provide and use puppets. There are many shapes, sizes, and types of puppets, from simple finger puppets to elaborate marionettes. We have provided several simple ways to create puppets for play. They are fun to use and are great tools for encouraging social interaction and language use.

Here are some ways to use puppets with students.

❶ **Start by just talking.** You may have to do the talking for two puppets, yours and the student's. Talk about school, home, favorite toys, and so on.

❷ **Practice a specific familiar sequence.** Repeat a song, nursery rhyme, poem, or TV jingle. Each puppet can say one line. Then have the puppets take turns.

❸ **Ask questions.** Have your puppet ask the student's puppet some easy questions that require only one- to three-word answers. At first, ask questions you are sure the student can answer.

❹ **Make the puppets interesting and exciting.** Use bright colors and textures that might appeal to students with autism (e.g., glitter, feathers, wiggly eyeballs, frizzy fabric, soft yarn).

Resources

Books
Hartigan, K. (1999). *Finger puppet mania.* St Louis, MO: Concordia.

Henson, C., Cain, D., & Barrett, J. E. (1994). *The muppets make puppets!* New York: Workman.

Ross, L. (1990). *Hand puppets: How to make and use them.* New York: Dover.

Web Sites
Aunt Annie's Crafts, Puppets Around the World: A Windows program for making several types of puppets. Instructions are provided for making a few of the puppets at this Web site. http://www.auntannie.com/puppets/index.html.

MTN Creekside Ent LLP: A source for individually made puppets. http://www.creekside-ent.com.

Pakaluk Puppets: Creators of lightweight hand puppets which are easy to manipulate, especially for children. http://www.Pakalukpuppets.com.

Playful Puppets: Unique puppets that can actually swallow objects. http://www.playfulpuppets.com.

Puppet People: Will make specially tailored puppets. http://ourworld.compuserve.com/homepages/stevekersys.

Puppet Artists: Individually designed and made puppets from fingerpuppets to marionettes. http://www.puppetartists.com.

Directions for Creating Stick Puppets

You can make simple stick puppets by following the directions below or using the patterns found on the next two pages. If you use the patterns, simply color, cut out, and glue them on a popsicle stick, dowel, plastic straw, or other suitable stick.

Styrofoam Ball Stick Puppets

Materials Needed
- two styrofoam balls, a small one for the head and a larger one for the body
- eyes
- colored pipe cleaners
- glue
- dowel
- felt, markers, yarn (optional)

Directions

1. Connect the two styrofoam balls together with three or four short pipe cleaners.
2. Use pipe cleaners to make arms and legs.
3. Glue eyes on small styrofoam ball.
4. Embellish by adding features such as mouth, hair or clothing using felt, markers, or yarn. This lets your audience know what the puppet is supposed to represent. You can make a wide variety of puppets this way, including humans and animals.
5. Connect the bottom of the body to the dowel.

Note. The patterns for stick puppets provided on this page are from *Practical Ideas That Really Work for Students with ADHD*, by Kathleen McConnell, Gail Ryser, and Judith Higgins, 2000, Austin, TX: PRO-ED, Inc. Copyright 2000 by PRO-ED, Inc. Reprinted with permission.

Idea 1

14

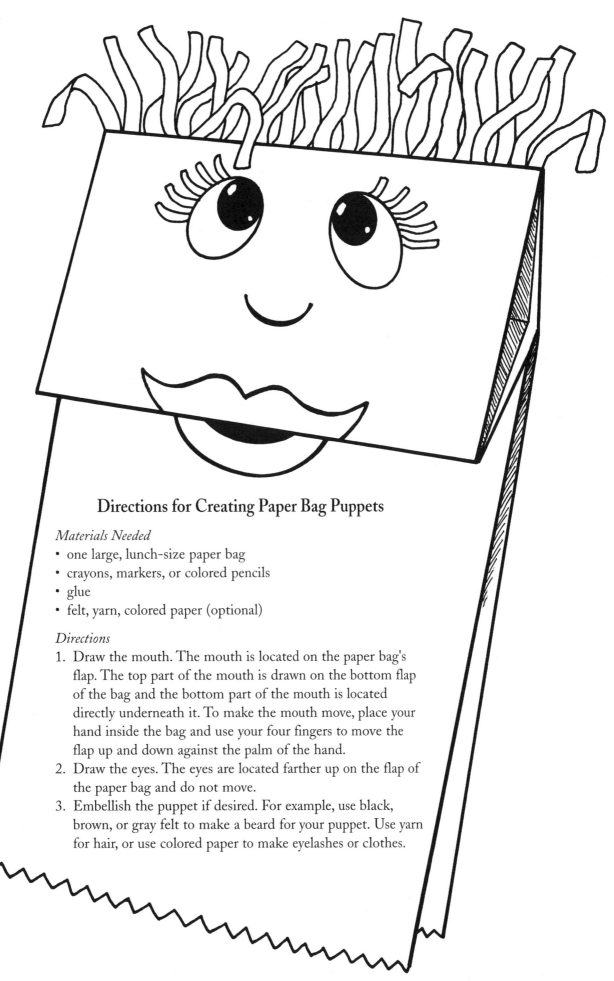

Directions for Creating Paper Bag Puppets

Materials Needed
- one large, lunch-size paper bag
- crayons, markers, or colored pencils
- glue
- felt, yarn, colored paper (optional)

Directions
1. Draw the mouth. The mouth is located on the paper bag's flap. The top part of the mouth is drawn on the bottom flap of the bag and the bottom part of the mouth is located directly underneath it. To make the mouth move, place your hand inside the bag and use your four fingers to move the flap up and down against the palm of the hand.
2. Draw the eyes. The eyes are located farther up on the flap of the paper bag and do not move.
3. Embellish the puppet if desired. For example, use black, brown, or gray felt to make a beard for your puppet. Use yarn for hair, or use colored paper to make eyelashes or clothes.

Idea 2
What To Teach Next

Students with autism spectrum disorders vary widely in their ability to function in their social and learning environments. The scale included with this book is one method you can use to implement intervention strategies to enable them to function more effectively. The skills in our scale are directly linked to the DSM–IV criteria and are broad in scope. It is also important to break skills down into more discrete tasks. For example, one item on our scale gives you information about a student's ability to use greetings or courteous phrases. However, you may want to know if there are conditions under which this same student uses speech and if so, what kind of speech. In addition, the DSM–IV does not specifically address academic skills, and it is important to know where to start academically for these children. The first step in determining what to teach next is to assess the student's current skills and deficiencies.

Several books provide guides that sequence academic, communication, motor, self-help, and other skills. (Two resources are listed below.) We have provided two handy forms; use the first one to assess the child and the second one to sequence and keep track of the skills to be taught.

☞ Tip:

Ask parents to assess their child or adolescent at home on the same skills to determine the degree of generalization. Give parents simple ways to follow through at home with the teaching of targeted skills.

Resources

Maurice, C. (Ed.), Green, G., & Luce, S. C. (Co-Eds.) (1996). *Behavioral intervention for young children with autism.* Austin, TX: PRO-ED.

Schopler, E., Lansing, M., & Waters, L. (Eds.) (1983). *Teaching activities for autsitc children.* Austin, TX: PRO-ED.

Here's how the Assessment form works.

❶ Determine the skill area in which you want to begin, for example, communication.

❷ Choose a skill from an existing hierarchy or develop your own hierarchy for that skill area and assess the child to determine mastery level. Make sure the skills you are assessing are developmentally appropriate for the student.

❸ Determine the first skill from the hierarchy to assess. Base this determination on what you already know the student can do in that skill area.

❹ Write the skill in the first box and write the observation time period in the second box on the form. Check off the settings in which the observation will occur. After observing, check the level at which the child is able to do the skill. In the last box on the form, check whether or not you are targeting that skill for intervention and write the beginning date.

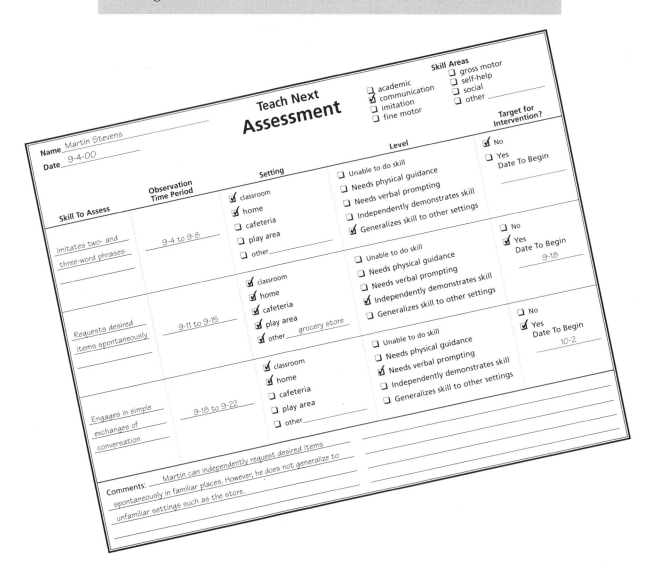

Name Martin Stevens
Date 9-4-00

Teach Next
Skills Progress

Skill Areas
- ☐ academic
- ☑ communication
- ☐ imitation
- ☐ fine motor
- ☐ gross motor
- ☐ self-help
- ☐ social
- ☐ other _____

Skill To Teach	Teaching Time Period	Setting	Materials Needed	Procedures	Level
Requests desired items spontaneously	9-18 to 9-29	☐ classroom ☐ home ☐ cafeteria ☐ play area ☑ other _store_	Auditory trainer (see Idea 23)	1. Teacher and Martin go to store to buy chips. 2. Martin enters store, teacher waits near doorway. 3. Teacher prompts as needed.	
Engages in simple exchanges of conversation	10-2 to 11-2	☑ classroom ☑ home ☐ cafeteria ☐ play area ☐ other _____	Talk Prompter Cards (see Idea 12) Puppets (see Idea 1)	1. Teacher and peer tutor model how to use the cards. 2. Martin and peer tutor practice using one card per week. 3. Teacher and Martin use puppets to simulate a conversation.	☐ Introduce ☐ Mastery ☑ Generalize
		☐ classroom ☐ home ☐ cafeteria ☐ play area ☐ other _____			☑ Introduce ☐ Mastery ☐ Generalize
					☐ Introduce ☐ Mastery ☐ Generalize

Comments: Martin will first work with the Talk Prompter Cards. As he progresses, the puppets will be used for reinforcement and to promote generalization.

Teach Next
Assessment

Name _____

Date _____

Skill Areas

- ☐ academic
- ☐ communication
- ☐ imitation
- ☐ fine motor
- ☐ gross motor
- ☐ self-help
- ☐ social
- ☐ other _____

Skill To Assess	Observation Time Period	Setting	Level	Target for Intervention?
_____ _____ _____	_____ _____	☐ classroom ☐ home ☐ cafeteria ☐ play area ☐ other_____	☐ Unable to do skill ☐ Needs physical guidance ☐ Needs verbal prompting ☐ Independently demonstrates skill ☐ Generalizes skill to other settings	☐ No ☐ Yes Date To Begin _____
_____ _____ _____	_____ _____	☐ classroom ☐ home ☐ cafeteria ☐ play area ☐ other_____	☐ Unable to do skill ☐ Needs physical guidance ☐ Needs verbal prompting ☐ Independently demonstrates skill ☐ Generalizes skill to other settings	☐ No ☐ Yes Date To Begin _____
_____ _____ _____	_____ _____	☐ classroom ☐ home ☐ cafeteria ☐ play area ☐ other_____	☐ Unable to do skill ☐ Needs physical guidance ☐ Needs verbal prompting ☐ Independently demonstrates skill ☐ Generalizes skill to other settings	☐ No ☐ Yes Date To Begin _____

Comments: _____
_____
_____

Idea 2

Teach Next
Skills Progress

Name _____

Date _____

Skill Areas

- ☐ academic
- ☐ communication
- ☐ imitation
- ☐ fine motor
- ☐ gross motor
- ☐ self-help
- ☐ social
- ☐ other _____

Skill To Teach	Teaching Time Period	Setting	Materials Needed	Procedures	Level
_____ _____ _____	_____ _____	☐ classroom ☐ home ☐ cafeteria ☐ play area ☐ other____	_____ _____ _____	_____ _____ _____	☐ Introduce ☐ Mastery ☐ Generalize
_____ _____ _____	_____ _____	☐ classroom ☐ home ☐ cafeteria ☐ play area ☐ other____	_____ _____ _____	_____ _____ _____	☐ Introduce ☐ Mastery ☐ Generalize
_____ _____ _____	_____ _____	☐ classroom ☐ home ☐ cafeteria ☐ play area ☐ other____	_____ _____ _____	_____ _____ _____	☐ Introduce ☐ Mastery ☐ Generalize

Comments: _____

_____

_____

Idea 3
Direct Teach Social Skills

There are many positive social behaviors that are essential in everyday situations. We often take for granted that students will learn these essential social skills by watching others, then imitating what they do. However, a student with autism or a related disorder may not learn as incidentally or as naturally as other students. Here are some social skills that you may need to teach through direct instruction, modeling, prompting, practice, and reinforcement. Whenever possible, teach these skills in the contexts in which they will be used (i.e., the locations and times they are needed as well as with the individuals who are normally present in the situations). Teaching essential skills may enable a student with autism to fit into a group, relate to peers, and avoid isolation.

Social Skills

Student _Chris Wilson_
Date: Week of _10-4-00_

Social Skill	Monday	Tuesday	Wednesday	Thursday	Friday
Where To Teach	greeting others	greeting others	greeting others	greeting others	greeting others
Who Will Teach	classroom	classroom	lunch room	office	classroom
How To Teach	Ms. Matthews	Ms. Matthews	peer tutor		
	☐ Explanation ☑ Demonstration ☑ Teacher Modeling ☐ Peer Modeling ☐ Prompts/Cues ☐ Guided Practice ☐ Independent Practice ☐ Other_____	☐ Explanation ☐ Demonstration ☑ Teacher Modeling ☐ Peer Modeling ☑ Prompts/Cues ☑ Guided Practice ☐ Independent Practice ☐ Other_____	☐ Explanation ☐ Demonstration ☐ Teacher Modeling ☑ Peer Modeling ☑ Prompts/Cues ☐ Guided Practice ☐ Independent Practice ☑ Other _prompted to greet lunch staff_	☐ Explanation ☐ Demonstration ☐ Teacher Modeling ☐ Peer Modeling ☐ Prompts/Cues ☑ Guided Practice ☑ Independent Practice ☑ Other _will greet office staff when sent on errand_	☐ Explanation ☐ Demonstration ☐ Teacher Modeling ☐ Peer Modeling ☐ Prompts/Cues ☐ Guided Practice ☑ Independent Practice ☑ Other _will greet her parents when picked up_
Evaluation Method	☐ Trial/Response Record ☑ Observation ☐ Product/Sample ☐ Other_____	☐ Trial/Response Record ☑ Observation ☐ Product/Sample ☐ Other_____	☐ Trial/Response Record ☑ Observation ☐ Product/Sample ☐ Other_____	☐ Trial/Response Record ☑ Observation ☐ Product/Sample ☑ Other _demonstrates skill with office staff_	☑ Trial/Response Record ☑ Observation ☐ Product/Sample ☑ Other _demonstrates skill with parents_
Homework	none	practice with parents at home			Chris to keep record of how many times she appropriately greets people over the weekend.

23

Following are some skills (with examples) that students with autism will likely need, but might not learn without being directly taught. When designing your instruction for these skills, you can use the Social Skills form provided.

Communicating

- Asking for something (scissors for cutting)

- Asking for help (when he or she can't reach an item)

- Greeting others (saying "hello" first)

- Joining a conversation (adding pertinent information to an ongoing discussion)

- Using courteous phrases ("please" and "thank you")

Waiting

- In line (cafeteria)

- For something to begin or end (a class activity)

- For meal time (not snacking or starting to eat until everyone is ready)

- For help (assistance with a difficult task)

- For a turn (playing with a toy)

Transitioning

- Following a schedule independently (especially a visual or pictorial schedule not requiring verbal reminders or prompts)

- Getting ready for an activity (locating garden tools needed for planting flowers)

- Cleaning up after an activity (putting dirty dishes in the dish washer

- Handing in a work product when completed (turning in a finished assignment)

- Moving from one scheduled service to another (going from speech therapy to P.E.)

Social Skills

Student _____

Date: Week of _____

	Monday	Tuesday	Wednesday	Thursday	Friday
Social Skill					
Where To Teach					
Who Will Teach					
How To Teach	☐ Explanation ☐ Demonstration ☐ Teacher Modeling ☐ Peer Modeling ☐ Prompts/Cues ☐ Guided Practice ☐ Independent Practice ☐ Other_____	☐ Explanation ☐ Demonstration ☐ Teacher Modeling ☐ Peer Modeling ☐ Prompts/Cues ☐ Guided Practice ☐ Independent Practice ☐ Other_____	☐ Explanation ☐ Demonstration ☐ Teacher Modeling ☐ Peer Modeling ☐ Prompts/Cues ☐ Guided Practice ☐ Independent Practice ☐ Other_____	☐ Explanation ☐ Demonstration ☐ Teacher Modeling ☐ Peer Modeling ☐ Prompts/Cues ☐ Guided Practice ☐ Independent Practice ☐ Other_____	☐ Explanation ☐ Demonstration ☐ Teacher Modeling ☐ Peer Modeling ☐ Prompts/Cues ☐ Guided Practice ☐ Independent Practice ☐ Other_____
Evaluation Method	☐ Trial/Response Record ☐ Observation ☐ Product/Sample ☐ Other_____	☐ Trial/Response Record ☐ Observation ☐ Product/Sample ☐ Other_____	☐ Trial/Response Record ☐ Observation ☐ Product/Sample ☐ Other_____	☐ Trial/Response Record ☐ Observation ☐ Product/Sample ☐ Other_____	☐ Trial/Response Record ☐ Observation ☐ Product/Sample ☐ Other_____
Homework					

Idea 3

Idea 4

Write Your Own: Social Skills Stories and Books

When students with autism or Asperger's disorder communicate best by reading and writing, follow their lead. To teach social skills, help students write their own stories and books that address problem social situations, then use their written lessons throughout the day as a personalized curriculum. Students can write stories and books to express wants, needs, and feelings or to suggest positive reactions to stressful situations.

Here's how to help students "write their own."

❶ With the student, choose a social situation that is problematic. If the student has good conversation skills, discuss which topics are most important to him and then let him select one. If your student is non-verbal or needs more structure, provide some visual examples of social situations as choices. The list below provides typical situations that require good social skills.

- What to do when your daily schedule changes

- How to wait your turn when you want something

- How to tell someone when you don't want to do something

- What to say if you are feeling sad (or angry, lonely, frustrated, happy, tired, sick, etc.)

- How to greet others

- How to join a group activity

- When and how to ask for something you want or to ask for assistance

- What to do if you don't get your own way or get what you want

- What to do if you are confused or lost

- How to tell someone you like them

❷ Next create a slot outline or story skeleton (or use either of the examples that we have provided) to help the student structure his story according to a consistent format. The first example provides one statement per page which the student illustrates. The second example located on page 36 has all of the statments on one page. The student may make illustrations at the bottom of the page in the boxes.

❸ Work with the student to write the story he dictates, assist him in filling in the blanks on the outline, or monitor as he writes his own story. If possible, use a computer to speed up the writing and editing process. As you and the student write, discuss appropriate and productive choices and responses to difficult social situations. Keep the story simple.

❹ After the social skills story is written, use it as a teaching tool. As the student completes more stories, use the stories as teaching tools, reminders, and discussion guides for social skills lessons.

❺ Collect all the student's stories and allow the student to publish his or her work as a completed book. We have provided easy-to-follow directions for designing and producing a book.

☞ Tip:

Use photographs of the student demonstrating positive social skills.

See Idea 5 for a variation on this idea.

Bookmaking and Binding Instructions

Method One

- Write the story on 6 by 9 inch pieces of colored paper.

- Laminate the paper.

- Staple together in the upper left-hand corner with the cover page on the front.

Method Two

- Write the story on 6 by 9 inch pieces of colored paper.

- Staple together along the left side of the pages.

- Cut two pieces of cardboard for the front and back covers of the book.

- Cut a piece of material or construction paper that is larger than the cardboard.

- Use dry mount to iron the book and the material to the cover or, if using construction paper, glue the construction paper to the cardboard.

- Decorate the cover.

Method Three

- Write the story on 6 by 9 inch pieces of colored paper.

- Decorate two pieces of cardboard for the front and back covers of the book. Place on flat surface with 3 to 4 inches of space between.

- Cut a piece of clear contact paper that is slightly larger than the cardboard.

- Fold the contact paper over the edges of the covers.

- Punch holes along the inside edges of the covers and the pages of the completed story.

- Put the pages of the story between the covers and use yarn or cord to lace the book together.

> ☞ **Tip:**
>
> For reinforcement, (before you cover the cardboard with contact paper) place masking tape along the edge of the cardboard where the holes will be punched.

How I Will Deal With

_____

By_____

1

This is hard for me: _____

_____ .

2

31

Idea 4

When this happens, I can say to myself, "_____

_____."

3

When this happens, I can do this: _____

_____.

4

I can ask _____ for help.

5

I can help myself remember by: _____

_____.

6

35

How I Will Deal With _____

　　　　　　By_____

1. Sometimes difficult situations can arise. For example, when _____

_____

_____ .

2. When this happens, I can deal with the situation by saying, "_____

_____

_____ "

and by doing this: _____

_____

_____ .

3. If I need help, I will ask _____ to help me.

4. To remind myself of what to do, I will _____

_____

_____ .

1	2	3	4

Idea 4

Idea 5
Read the Sign

Here's a variation on Idea 4. Instead of using books, use portable signs.

Here are some ways to use signs.

❶ To indicate scheduled events or activities

❷ To alert the student to changes or transitions

❸ To prepare the student for dealing with difficult situations

❹ To provide explicit directions or examples that help the student communicate with others

---

We have provided two examples of basic signs that can be used after pertinent information is filled in the blanks. However, we suggest that you not limit yourself to these two suggestions. Consider involving the student in writing his or her own signs or filling in the blanks as a way of problem solving and processing information.

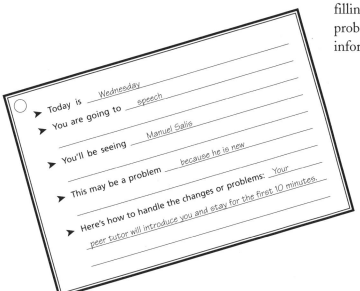

➤ Today is ___Wednesday___

➤ You are going to ___speech___

➤ You'll be seeing ___Manuel Salis___

➤ This may be a problem ___because he is new___

➤ Here's how to handle the changes or problems: ___Your peer tutor will introduce you and stay for the first 10 minutes.___

☞ **Tip:**

The signs are great for students to carry with them throughout the day. Laminate them, punch a hole in the top left corner, and put them on a ring or key chain so they are portable and easy to modify.

○

➤ Today is _____

➤ You are going to _____
_____

➤ You'll be seeing _____
_____

➤ This may be a problem _____
_____

➤ Here's how to handle the changes or problems: _____
_____
_____

○

➤ Today is _____

➤ Today it might be difficult to _____
_____

➤ When this happens, you can say this: _____
_____

➤ And do this: _____
_____

➤ Help yourself get ready for stressful situations by _____
_____
_____

Idea 5

Idea 6
Your Turn/My Turn

Students with autism spectrum disorders often have deficits in the areas of social interaction and language use. Both of these domains can be addressed by structuring situations that encourage turn taking and reciprocal interactions. Here's how to begin the process.

❶ First brainstorm a list of age-appropriate activities that two people can do together and easily take turns. Examples include:
- Building something with blocks
- Completing a puzzle
- Setting the table or stacking dishes
- Turning an appliance or the lights off and on
- Kicking a soccer ball back and forth
- Playing a simple card game like Uno or war
- Filling a glass and then emptying it
- Turning the pages of a book
- Coloring a picture or painting a page with water
- Clicking a computer mouse
- Dropping items into a bucket or plastic tub
- Singing a repeated phrase or clapping in rhythm

❷ Next decide on a logical sequence of language to use while doing the activity. Think of words that make sense when used in the context of the activity and are easy to repeat and remember. Use the phrases each time you do the activity. Then pause and wait for the student to repeat after you. Use special encouragement for using pronouns correctly, since this can be problematic for students with autism. Some examples include:
- *My* turn. Now *your* turn.
- *Mine. Yours.*
- First *you* (or the student's name, First *Bobby*). Then *me* (or your name, Then *Mrs. Jones*).
- *You* go. Now *I* go.
- Now *you*. Now *me*.
- Whose turn? That's right, *Sally's* turn.

❸ Finally, reinforce the student with enthusiastic praise every time he or she takes a turn. Use even more enthusiasm if the language that you have modeled is used.

Idea 7

Nice Looking

Lack of eye contact is one of the defining characteristics of autism or Asperger's syndrome. It is important that students make eye contact with others so that they begin the socialization process and let others know they are paying attention.

To increase eye contact, try these ideas.

❶ If you are teaching by direct instruction and are facing the student, hold up a colorful or enticing object right next to your eye. This will encourage the student to move his or her eyes in the right direction.

❷ Consistently use the same verbal direction to request the student to look, regardless of the situation. Throughout the day, whether in the hall, the cafeteria, or at a job site, using the same words will help the student learn to make eye contact more quickly.

❸ Get excited! Your tone of voice and level of enthusiasm are very important. Use the student's name, say "hello," wave, and point to your eyes. Do all you can to focus attention.

❹ For a student who has already learned to make eye contact and just needs to maintain this skill, positive reinforcement after he or she looks at you is the key to success. Simple, clear comments like "good looking" or "nice eye contact" will help, along with consistent use of the *I Saw Your Eyes* coupons. The coupons can be exchanged for positive reinforcers from a menu. (See Idea 35.)

I Saw Your Eyes

Nice Looking!

I Saw Your Eyes

Nice Looking!

I Saw Your Eyes

Nice Looking!

Idea 8
Learn To Imitate; Imitate To Learn

One of the most basic ways to learn how to do something is to watch others and then do what they do. For students with autism or related disorders, teaching students to imitate is a good instructional strategy. This is especially true for very young students with an autism spectrum disorder, since we are trying to establish imitation as a way of learning. The individual behaviors students imitate are sometimes not as important as the cognitive connection they make ("Oh, look what he is doing. I can do that too," or "She said this. I'll say it too."). We hope that students not only learn to imitate the actions and language of others in structured teaching situations, but that they also begin to imitate what they see or hear throughout the day.

You can teach through imitation by beginning with physical movements. Later you can teach communication through gestures, signs, and words. We have provided some basic gross motor imitations to use with students who need to learn how to imitate and/or who are very young. You can make these motor imitations more fun by providing cues or interesting names.

Here are some imitations to use.

- Marching (to music or a drum)

- Clapping hands (applause, "Good job")

- Standing up and sitting down (perhaps as a "Simon Says" direction)

- Stomping feet (walk like an elephant)

- Raising arms above one's head (cheering)

- Throwing a kiss (movie star kisses)

- Touching a body part (start with the most obvious first (e.g., head, tummy, nose, mouth, feet)

- Waving ("Bye-bye")

- Jumping or hopping (sometimes on one foot, sometimes with both feet)

- "High fives" (first with two hands, then one at a time)

- Hugging (everyone's favorite)

☞ Tip:

❶ Follow each successful imitation with lots of praise and reinforcement.

❷ Keep track of which imitations the student has mastered, then move on to a new skill.

Idea 9
Get Excited

Many students with autism spectrum disorders fail to react with enjoyment, interest, or excitement, even in situations or activities that you know they like. Although it is difficult to teach, showing enthusiasm or interest is an important social skill because it connects students to others, is part of the communication process, and indicates students' awareness of their environment.

One strategy for teaching a student to demonstrate pleasure, interest, enjoyment, or excitement is a 2-step procedure involving a prompt, then a reinforcer. Our idea has an extra bonus because the prompt itself is part of the reinforcer.

Here's how the plan works.

❶ The first step is to select an object (toy, food, or drink), activity (listening to a CD, playing a game, or looking at a magazine), or person (Grandma, brother, or friend) that you are absolutely certain the student likes a lot. As you introduce the object, activity, or person, prompt the student by:
  • modeling excitement ("Wow, look who's here!");
  • gesturing (giving a thumbs-up when chocolate ice cream appears); or
  • physically prompting (guiding the student's hands to clap for a CD he likes).

After the prompt and verbal encouragement to respond ("This is great! Now show me how excited you are by _____."), wait briefly for a response. If the student doesn't show you an enthusiastic response, repeat the prompt and show the object, activity, or person again.

❷ At the first sign of excitement reinforce the student immediately by:
  • giving him the object, beginning the preferred activity, or letting him spend time with his favorite person; and
  • demonstrating your own enthusiasm by clapping, patting, hugging, praising, and/or cheering.

In order to maximize chances for success, use reinforcers that are highly valued and preferred by the student. You will know what to pick if you observe the student carefully, or let him create his own excitement menu.

We have provided a form to accompany this idea. The teacher should use the left side of the form in the teaching process, both to set criteria and to explain what is required. The right side of the form is the menu of reinforcers, which can be changed periodically.

Directions for Completing the Form

On the left side of the form, check off one of the boxes to indicate how you would like the student to respond. This will be the action you demonstrate for the student. On the right side of the form, write, draw, or place photos of the student's reinforcers. Check the reinforcers that are available during each practice session.

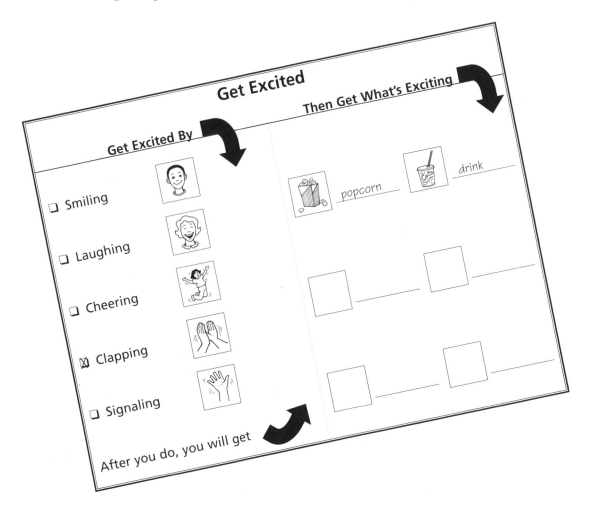

Get Excited

Get Excited By

- ☐ Smiling
- ☐ Laughing
- ☐ Cheering
- ☐ Clapping
- ☐ Signaling

After you do, you will get

Then Get What's Exciting

These Objects

These Activities

These People

Idea 9

47

Idea 10
Follow the Music

Music can enrich lives and is a great resource to use with students with autism and other pervasive developmental disabilities. Music is used to teach skills, improve relaxation, and decrease repetitive, stereotyped behaviors. This idea presents four simple ways to use music.

Playing music, especially songs with action words, can improve a student's receptive language. Many songs require participants to respond to simple commands. Some of these include "The Hokey Pokey"; "Head, Shoulders, Knees, and Toes"; "Open–Shut"; and "I'm a Little Teapot." Older students will enjoy simple rap songs.

Here are three music books that contain songs that use simple commands or physical actions.

Glazer, T., & Lazarevich, M. (1980). *Do your ears hang low?* Garden City, NY: Doubleday.

Hart, J., & Lobel, A. (1982). *Singing bee!* New York: Lothrop, Lee & Shepard.

Nelson, E. L., & Behr, J. (1981). *The silly song-book.* New York: Sterling.

In addition, music can be used to prompt students to specific actions. For example, use a simple melody to signal students to put away their work. Use a different melody to signal students to line up quietly to go to lunch.

Another use of music is to help students learn to imitate movements. While students listen and watch, make simple movements and sway to the music. Now prompt your students to imitate you. Use objects, such as toys or clothing, to make it more interesting.

Finally, music can have a calming effect. One method used by some professionals that helps students with autism and other pervasive developmental disabilities to relax and decrease repetitive, stereotyped behaviors and aggression, is called rhythmic entrainment intervention. This method uses rhythms that are specifically designed to produce 50 to 65 beats per minute.

These Web sites provide additional information about rhythmic entrainment intervention.

http://www.reiinstitute.com (800/659-6644)

http://www.healthysounds.com

Idea 11
Step-By-Step

Teaching a student with autism to accept or tolerate physical contact is often difficult; yet, this is one of the DSM-IV indicators of the disorder. Sometimes, increasing a student's tolerance for closeness or for touch requires a step-by-step approach while the student is engaged in an enjoyable activity.

Here are some ideas.

Use Water

Encourage the student to play in the water at a sink or water table. While he is playing, stand across from the student, lightly rippling the water and splashing gently. While the student's hands and your hands are both in the water, touch the student's hands lightly for brief periods of time. As time goes on, begin extending the touch time by playing with boats and other floating objects with the student.

Play in Sand or with Clay or Shaving Cream

Provide modeling or synthetic clay, sand, or shaving cream for students, until you find a texture that the student prefers. (One caution here: If the student is likely to put any of these in his mouth, find another medium). While the student plays, put your hands in the sand, clay, or cream, wiggling your fingers, gently sifting the sand, or helping the student mold an object. While assisting the student, gently touch his hands for brief periods of time, extending this time as the student grows more comfortable.

Use Everyday Gestures

An easy way to help students get comfortable with touch is to use everyday touches that communicate. Gestures like "high fives," handshakes, hugs, and pats on the back communicate approval, enjoyment, and encouragement; they not only increase tolerance for touch but can be reinforcing as well. Encourage parents to use encouraging touches often.

For Older Students

If you want to continue to encourage students to tolerate touch even when they are older, consider these additional ideas:

• Take turns playing electronic or video games, with button or stick controllers. Guide the student's hands by lightly placing your hand over his.

• Use musical instruments to encourage touching. For example, playing the piano together can help students if you gradually increase your physical guidance.

• The computer mouse is a great tool. Students often need assistance and will tolerate physical touch because they enjoy the computer games or programs so much.

• Don't forget shared reading. Whether you are looking at a magazine or reading a book, you can take turns turning pages and pointing to pictures, as well as sitting close to each other.

Idea 12
Talk Prompters

Students with autism spectrum disorders are often poor at initiating and maintaining conversation. Use the Talk Prompters to teach students how to begin and extend a conversation. The Talk Prompters on the following pages are designed to be used as conversation openers and extenders, and can be used to teach these important communication skills.

Each card is designed to be two-sided. (Copy the Opener Cards on one side, and copy the Extender Cards on the other side.) One side is called the Opener and has an O at the top of the card. The other side is called the Extender and has an E at the top of the card. Each side has a prompt (word phrase) followed by a blank. Below the blank are several words or word phrases that can be placed into the blank.

Here's how to use Talk Prompters.

❶ First, take any card and turn it to the Opener side. For example: The "What's your favorite _____?" prompt is followed by four suggestions: dessert, TV show, game, time of day. Model for the students how to take each word or word phrase and complete the question.

❷ Next turn the card over to the Extender side. Model for the students how to extend the conversation by repeating the phrase.

❸ Then group the students in pairs to practice using the prompts. Try using one prompt per week.

☞ **Tip:**

Copy, laminate, and place the cards on a small ring. Give each student a set. Group the students in pairs and let them practice.

Opener Cards

What's your favorite _____? O
- TV show
- dessert
- game
- animal

What do you do when you are _____? O
- scared
- happy
- excited
- sad

What did you _____? O
- eat for lunch
- do today
- learn in school this week
- do for fun last night

What is the name of _____? O
- your best friend
- the city you live in
- your teacher at school
- the school you go to

Where did you go _____? O
- for the weekend
- last night
- for your birthday
- after school

Where could I go to _____? O
- find a good book
- buy groceries
- play a game
- get an ice-cream cone

Idea 12

Extender Cards

Do you like feeling _____?
- scared
- happy
- excited
- sad

E

What do you like best about your favorite _____?
- TV show
- dessert
- game
- animal

E

What is one thing you like about _____?
- your best friend
- the city you live in
- your teacher at school
- the school you go to

E

Did you like what you _____?
- ate for lunch
- did today
- learned in school this week
- did for fun last night

E

How do I get to the place where I could _____?
- find a good book
- buy groceries
- play a game
- get an ice-cream cone

E

What did you do _____?
- for the weekend
- last night
- for your birthday
- after school

E

Idea 12

Idea 13
Get Predictable

We know that learning to use language in reading, writing, and talking is an interactive process. One strategy for encouraging students to improve their language skills is to use predictable or patterned books. Predictable books are usually colorful, engaging, and fun to read, so they are a great motivator for students with any level of language proficiency. These patterned books provide students with autism spectrum disorders an extra bonus: an opportunity for social interaction while taking turns reading with their teacher.

Using the books is easy.

• Sit close.

• Read aloud.

• Frequently omit a word or phrase and wait for the student to "fill in the blank" by saying the missing word or phrase.

Make things even more challenging.

• Ask students to identify people and things in the pictures.

• Point to pictures to identify objects.

• Repeat aloud what you have read.

Since many students with autism spectrum disorders are good at repeating what they hear, this process is a natural fit for their learning style. Two examples of patterned or predictable books are *Brown Bear, Brown Bear* by Bill Martin and *Where the Wild Things Are* by Maurice Sendak. For a list of 200 patterned books, see *Reading as Communication: An Interactive Approach*, 3rd ed. (pp. 566–569), by Frank B. May, 1990, New York: Macmillan.

Idea 14
Take One and Pass It On

Students with autism spectrum disorders often lack effective social interaction skills. They frequently fail to develop peer relationships and have problems sharing, enjoying activities with others, and taking turns. Here is a small group activity that requires students to practice these key social skills. Before beginning with the group, it may be necessary to teach some of the verbal or physical actions to students in one-to-one situations. Practice the words and movements ahead of time so that the group interactions are more natural.

Here's how to structure Take One and Pass It On.

❶ Before beginning, fill a container (basket, plastic bowl, tray, or box) with individual items. You might want to start with food items like pretzels, raisins, crackers, apple or pear slices, or cereal; you can eventually use other objects like photographs, small puzzles, or pencils and small pads of paper.

❷ Have students sit in a circle either on chairs or on the floor.

❸ Hand the student next to you the container. As you hand it to the student, say his or her name and the direction. For example, "Here, Alec, have a pretzel and pass it on."

❹ Cue the student to respond as you have already taught him, perhaps by saying, "Thanks."

❺ Then, cue him to look at the next person in the circle, pass the container, and say, "Here, have a pretzel and pass it on." If possible, have the student include the person's name.

❻ Reinforce students each time they respond correctly.

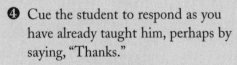

For students who do not use verbal language, focus your teaching and reinforcement on the physical social skills involved, including sitting close to others, making eye contact, taking an object from someone else, and passing it on to the next person. Students who have good oral language can be encouraged to use their language naturally and fluently. Saying "thanks" and using other students' names are positive and important skills they can practice during this activity.

☞ **Tip:**

When beginning this activity, it may be necessary to have an adult sit behind or next to some students to guide or assist them with the physical actions involved.

Idea 15

Conversation Cards

Many students with autism or related disorders need to improve their language and social skills in everyday social situations. Whether greeting someone, asking introductory questions, sharing information, or just making polite conversation, it helps if students know about the people in their lives, including the person's name and something about him or her (e.g., occupation, hobby, family information).

To help prepare a student for conversation, create a card file.

Each card can provide a name, photo, and basic information about a friend, classmate, coworker, family member, neighbor, teacher, bus driver, therapist, or acquaintance. Use the cards to teach and prepare students *before* they encounter people in social situations. Students can practice saying names, greetings, asking and answering relevant questions, and saying "goodbye."

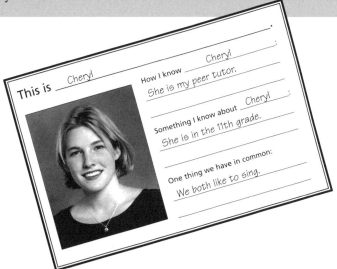

This is _____.

(photo)

How I know _____:

_____

_____

Something I know about _____:

_____

_____

One thing we have in common:

_____

_____

This is _____.

(photo)

How I know _____:

_____

_____

Something I know about _____:

_____

_____

One thing we have in common:

_____

_____

62

Idea 16
Bring Out the Noise

When small children learn to talk, they begin by making sounds like laughter, cries, or single sounds that do not really have meaning. These vocalizations serve an important purpose, because they provide a basis for reciprocal interaction. Parents and caregivers often mimic and repeat the child's sounds while smiling, tickling, and touching the child.

When students with autism are nonverbal, it can be difficult for teachers to stimulate them to make noises, small sounds, or laughter. However, encouraging vocalizations is important so that students begin the language development process.

Here are some ways to bring out the noise.

❶ Tickling the student

❷ Blowing bubbles, especially near the student's face

❸ Playing music or musical instruments

❹ Playing hide-and-seek or peek-a-boo

❺ Repeating rhymes and chants, along with gestures and movements

❻ Talking through puppets

❼ Hugging, swinging, or gently lifting the student into the air

☞ Tip:

As soon as you hear the student make some sounds, repeat them back to the student, then clap praise, cheer, smile, and make a big fuss to encourage the student to say more.

Idea 17
Talk Back Cards

Encouraging students with autism spectrum disorders to engage in meaningful back-and-forth conversation can sometimes be difficult. This lack of conversation impacts both social relationships and opportunities to learn and practice language skills. One way to help students get started with conversations is to use Talk Back Cards.

We have provided three types of Talk Back Cards for people, places, and things. The blanks on the cards can be filled in with words, photographs, or symbols representing people, places, and things familiar to the student. Each card has a simple two-part conversation.

The repetitive nature of the cards should make the student's learning easier, but don't limit the student's responses to just what the cards say, especially if he or she is expanding the content of the conversation.

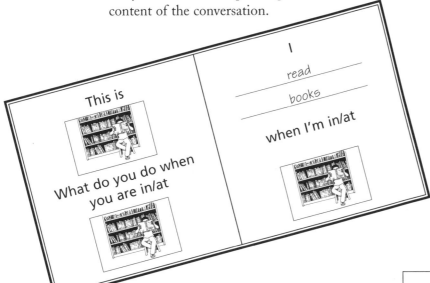

> ☞ **Tip:**
>
> To help keep the student focused on one part of the conversation at a time, you may want to fold the card and show only one half at a time.

Here's how to use the Talk Back Cards.

1. Begin the conversation by reading the left side of the card, emphasizing the name of the person, place, or thing.

2. Next prompt the student to respond by showing him the right side of the card. If necessary, read it yourself first, and then encourage the student to repeat what you have said.

3. After the student can repeat his part of the conversation, encourage generalization by
   - eliminating the cards;
   - expanding on the conversation by adding details; or
   - having the student initiate the conversation instead of responding.

This is

(name or photo
of a person the
student knows)

How do you know

(same name or photo)

(same name or photo)

is my

_____

This is

(name or photo
of a person the
student knows)

How do you know

(same name or photo)

(same name or photo)

is my

_____

Idea 17

This is

(word, photo, or symbol representing a place the student is familiar with)

What do you do when you are in/at

(same name, photo, or symbol)

I

_____

_____

when I'm in/at

(same name, photo, or symbol)

This is

(word, photo, or symbol representing a place the student is familiar with)

What do you do when you are in/at

(same name, photo, or symbol)

I

_____

_____

when I'm in/at

(same name, photo, or symbol)

Idea 17

This is a

(word, photo, or symbol representing a thing the student is familiar with)

What do you do with a

(same name, photo, or symbol)

I

_____

_____

with a

(same name, photo, or symbol)

This is a

(word, photo, or symbol representing a thing the student is familiar with)

What do you do with a

(same name, photo, or symbol)

I

_____

_____

with a

(same name, photo, or symbol)

Idea 17

Idea 18
Choice Cards

Students with autism spectrum disorders often fail to indicate their preference or interest in daily activities or everyday objects. This lack of enthusiasm and communication may isolate students from their peers and family members. One simple way to help students begin the process of sharing their interests is to teach them to indicate their choice of two or more options. By making choices, students begin to express preferences and learn the importance of communciation: They will get what they want more often if they make a choice.

Choice Cards are a simple tool to help you teach students to express a preference or make a choice. The teacher structures the choices, and then students are required to select what they want. Use the cards on the following pages throughout the day to encourage students tell you what they want to do, where they would like to go, what they want to eat or drink, how they are feeling, when they want to go somewhere, etc. After students make a choice between two options, begin to expand to three or four options. Fill in the blanks with photographs, symbols (like those from the Mayer-Johnson Company), simple drawings, words, phrases, or any combination of these.

☞ Tip:

If you use photos or symbols, attach fasteners to the front of the Choice Cards and also to the back of the pictures, so that you can change the choice selections often. If you are writing words on the Choice Cards, laminate the cards so that you can wipe them off whenever you switch activities.

Order Information for Mayer-Johnson Company

Picture Communication Symbols (PCS). A set of 3200 picture symbols used for communication.

Boardmaker software (Macintosh and Windows). Creates communication displays.

Mayer-Johnson Company
P.O. Box 1579
Solana Beach, CA 92075
Phone 800/588-4548
Fax 858/550-0449
http://www.mayer-johnson.com

What do you want to

_____ ? _____ or _____

Where do you want to

_____ ? _____ or _____

Who do you want to

_____ ? _____ or _____

When do you want to

_____ ? _____ or _____

How do you want to

_____ ? _____ or _____

73

Idea 19
The Daily Scoop

All parents and teachers want to be able to communicate with their children or students. Sharing information, whether about school or home, builds relationships and provides a basis for improving language skills. In addition, a good home–school communication system helps ensure that everyone knows what is happening in a student's life and should prevent misunderstandings.

The Daily Scoop provides an easy to use, convenient format for home–school communication. You can use any one of several formats to help students share what they have done, where they have gone, whom they have seen, and so on. Teachers and parents can send these back and forth daily. We hope that the convenient format will ensure their consistent use.

The Daily Scoop

Date_____

At home I:

_____

_____

_____

Idea 19

The Daily Scoop

Directions: Use pictures, symbols, or words to communicate the events that occurred at school.

Date_____

At school I:

_____

_____

_____

Idea 19

The Daily Scoop

Directions: Create a menu of pictures, symbols, or words that can be circled by the student each day.

Date_____

Today I ate:

orange

raisins

cookie

pizza

sandwich

chips

Today I went to these classes:

Reading

Music

P. E.

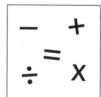
Math

Today I saw these people:

my teacher

the bus driver

my friend

Idea 19

The Daily Scoop

Directions: Create a menu of pictures, symbols, or words that can be circled by the student each day.

Date_____

Today I ate:

Today I went to these classes:

Today I saw these people:

Idea 19

Idea 20

Yes/No Cards

Indicating a yes/no response is an important skill for students. Whether they do so physically (with a head nod or a head shake), verbally (by saying the words "yes" or "no"), or by another method (pushing a red or green button or light, using a signal, etc.), the important lesson for students is that their meaningful use of some form of language produce a result. The more often a student gets what he or she wants by indicating "yes" or "no," the more likely he or she may be to use language consistently and often. Here's a strategy for students who are nonverbal.

Throughout the day, frequently ask the student questions that require a yes/no response. Teach and guide the student to respond by pointing to either the green Yes card or the red No card. Immediately after the student responds, honor the request. For example, if you ask, "Do you want a drink?" and the student points to Yes, provide him or her with a drink as quickly as you can. If the student indicates No, don't force a drink just because you think he or she needs one.

☞ **Tips:**

❶ Make sure you don't ask yes/no questions that you can't or won't honor. The point is to teach students that using language will get them what they want.

❷ Copy the Yes cards on green paper and the No cards on red paper and laminate before using.

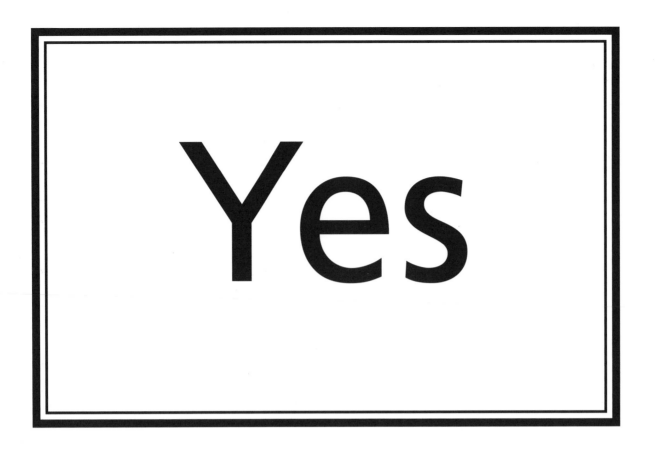

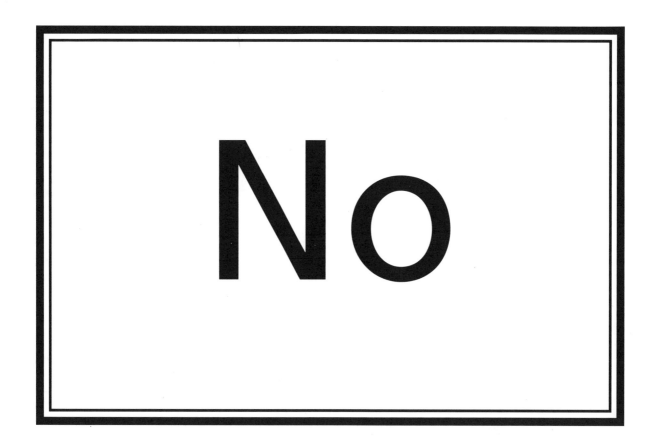

No

No	No
No	No

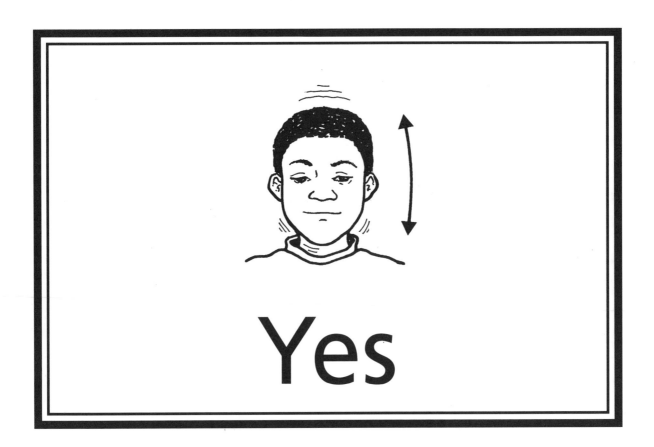

Yes

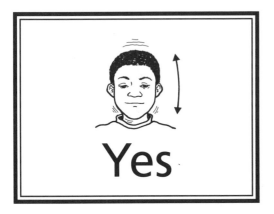

Yes

Yes

Yes

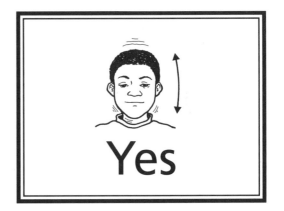

Yes

Idea 20

No

No

No

No

No

Idea 20

Idea 21

"I" Cue Card

Many students with autism use speech patterns that include echolalia. In echolalic speech, the student repeats what he has heard rather then responding meaningfully with the pronoun *I*. The following is an example:

Mrs. Jones: "Hi, Billy, how are you?"

Billy: "Hi, Billy, how are you?"

instead of

"I'm fine, thank you."

To encourage students to use the pronoun *I* and respond to others' questions and comments, try this two-step process:

❶ After asking the student a question, pause, then say the word "I" while holding up the "I" Cue Card.

❷ If the student repeats the *I*, model the rest of the response. (As in the example above, "I'm fine.") Then wait again for the student's response.

Gradually phase out your verbal modeling and just use the "I" Cue Card as a visual prompt. Hopefully you will one day be able to phase out the cue card as well.

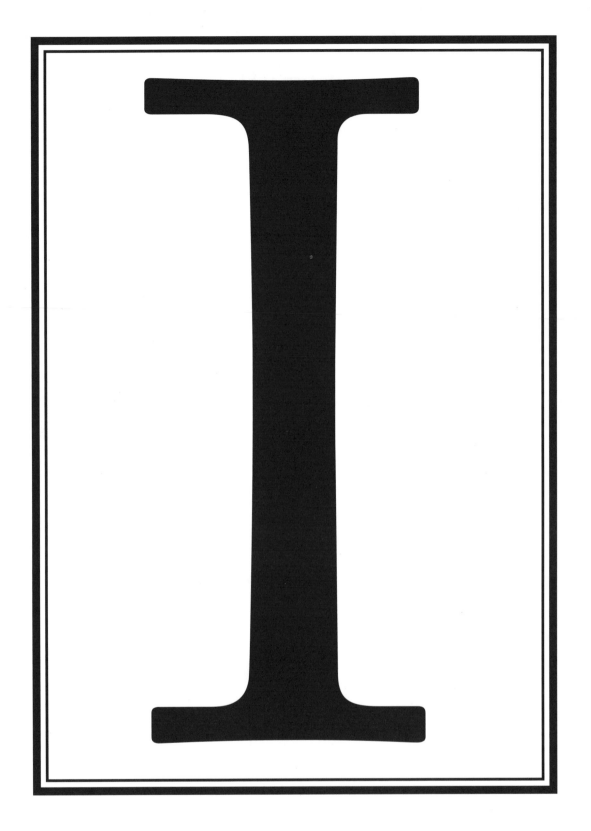

Idea 21

Idea 22
Subtle Sabotage

It is important that adults not anticipate all of a student's needs and then meet them without first encouraging the student to communicate. One way to maximize students' opportunities to use language is to "sabotage," or structure situations that are out of the ordinary, difficult, incorrect, or require assistance. In these situations, students are encouraged to communicate more often and more naturally.

Here are some ways to set up a student to communicate.

❶ When the student indicates that he wants something, purposefully give him something else (a *wrong* item), or pretend you don't understand.

❷ Give the student something he really wants, but put it in a see-through container like a plastic bag or jar that he cannot open by himself.

❸ Tightly fasten the lid of a container the student wants opened, so that he will need help.

❹ If the student wants to wash his hands or play in water, stand in front of the sink but *forget* to turn on the tap.

❺ When leaving a room with the student, walk to the door; then wait and don't open it for him.

❻ Leave out a step when following a common routine (e.g., leave the lights off instead of turning them on after entering the room).

❼ Give the student a tray in the cafeteria, but don't put the food or drink on it for him.

❽ Put a favorite toy out of reach on a high shelf so the student has to ask for it.

❾ Put something in the wrong place (a chair in the middle of the aisle), or hold something the wrong way (an upside down book).

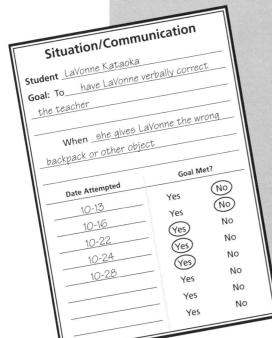

Situation/Communication

Student __LaVonne Kataoka__

Goal: To __have LaVonne verbally correct__
__the teacher__

When __she gives LaVonne the wrong__
__backpack or other object__

Date Attempted	Goal Met?	
10-13	Yes	(No)
10-16	Yes	(No)
10-22	(Yes)	No
10-24	(Yes)	No
10-28	(Yes)	No
	Yes	No
	Yes	No
	Yes	No

If your sabotage works, and the student initiates communication, make sure that you respond by requiring as much language as possible and then praising the student. Whenever possible, talk through the situation. (e.g., Say, "Oh my, we forgot to put juice in your glass. What do we need?" Wait for the word *juice*, then say, "That's right, juice. Good for you!") If you know that a student can say a particular word but does not use it consistently, use this strategy to set up a contingency. (If you say "juice," you get *juice*.) Keep a record of the student's progress on the Situation/Communication form provided.

Situation/Communication

Student _____

Goal: To_____

_____

_____

When _____

_____

_____

Date Attempted	Goal Met?	
_____	Yes	No
_____	Yes	No
_____	Yes	No
_____	Yes	No
_____	Yes	No
_____	Yes	No
_____	Yes	No
_____	Yes	No

Situation/Communication

Student _____

Goal: To_____

_____

_____

When _____

_____

_____

Date Attempted	Goal Met?	
_____	Yes	No
_____	Yes	No
_____	Yes	No
_____	Yes	No
_____	Yes	No
_____	Yes	No
_____	Yes	No
_____	Yes	No

Situation/Communication

Student _____

Goal: To_____

_____

_____

When _____

_____

_____

Date Attempted	Goal Met?	
_____	Yes	No
_____	Yes	No
_____	Yes	No
_____	Yes	No
_____	Yes	No
_____	Yes	No
_____	Yes	No
_____	Yes	No

Situation/Communication

Student _____

Goal: To_____

_____

_____

When _____

_____

_____

Date Attempted	Goal Met?	
_____	Yes	No
_____	Yes	No
_____	Yes	No
_____	Yes	No
_____	Yes	No
_____	Yes	No
_____	Yes	No
_____	Yes	No

Idea 22

Idea 23
Teacher Prompts, Student Talks

Students with Asperger's disorder or autism frequently master the mechanics of spoken language but have difficulty using their language fluently and naturally in conversations. They may have problems beginning, continuing, or ending the conversation and, consequently, their language sounds stilted or robotic. One way to support a student with poor conversation skills is to set up situations with others that require normal conversation and then support the student by talking him or her through the process. The unique feature of our prompting strategy is that, thanks to technology like the auditory trainer used in this idea, the teacher doesn't need to be close to the student to do the prompting. We hope that allowing the student to converse without the teacher being physically present will encourage him or her to use language smoothly and spontaneously in social situations. The teacher should gradually prompt less and less until the student carries on a back-and-forth conversation independently.

Here's how Teacher Prompts, Student Talks works.

❶ First make sure the student is wearing his earphone.

❷ Next arrange a typical situation for the student. For example, an older student might be in a store, buying snack food.

❸ As the student begins the process of purchasing his snack, the teacher, who is out of sight of the student (perhaps off to the side or behind a display rack), waits to see if the student needs some support or if he can handle the conversation alone.

❹ If the student is having trouble getting started, the teacher prompts him by softly speaking into his microphone. Using normal conversational words and tone, the teacher will suggest a conversation opener. (For example, "Hi. I'd like to buy this bag of chips." or "Hello. How are you today?")

❺ The student, hearing the prompt through his earphone, repeats the opener.

❻ The conversation should then proceed with back-and-forth talking until the student has completed his purchase, ending perhaps with a "thank you" and "good-bye."

☞ Tip:

It is important not to prompt too often or with too many words. Only offer words when the student is stuck or having problems responding naturally and begin with simple words and phrases, so the student feels comfortable and gains confidence.

Sources for Auditory Trainers

Earmark, Inc.	Phonic Ear	Telex Communications, Inc.
1125 Dixwell Ave.	3880 Cypress Drive	9600 Aldrich Avenue South
Hamden, CT 06514	Petaluma, CA 94954-7600	Minneapolis, MN 55420
Tel. 888/327-6275	Tel. 800/227-0735	Tel. 612/884-4051
Fax 203/777-2886	Fax 707/769-9624	Fax 612/884-0043
http://www.earmark.com	http://www.phonicear.com	http://www.telex.com

Idea 24
Great Games

Games are a great way of teaching many different skills. For students with autism spectrum disorders, active games can address a variety of needs in problematic areas. Games help students autism in several skill areas, including building social relationships, sharing enjoyment, improving turn-taking skills, reducing their social isolation, and using language in meaningful ways. These games, many of which are classics, allow students and teachers to move, laugh, and have fun together while they address these important skills. Try using these and other games as the basis for teaching to specific objectives.

Here are some great games to play.

- Peek-a-Boo
- Pat-a-Cake
- Ring Around the Rosey
- Musical Chairs
- Ring or Frisbee Toss
- Croquet
- Basketball

- Catch
- Hide-and-Seek
- Red Light/Green Light
- Checkers
- I Spy
- Computer Games for Two
- Statue

☞ Tip:

As you play, talk the students through the game, require turn taking, and demonstrate your own enthusiasm.

One good game for building and improving language skills is Guess What. This game is a simple version of a childhood guessing game sometimes called, "I'm thinking of something . . . ."

The turn taking in Guess What is important because it builds back-and-forth conversation skills. The clues provided in the game are important because they encourage students to think about the function, characteristics, and similarities of objects. These are important aspects of language and concept development.

Here's how Guess What works.

❶ Whenever a few minutes are available and the student is not engaged in a lesson, provide some clues and get the guessing started by saying,

> "I'm thinking of something that is _____ (say a color such as red, green, or yellow) and _____ (say the function such as we see at the corner, has pretty flowers, or we peel and eat). Guess what it is."

❷ If the student responds correctly, compliment him or her for good thinking and talking. Make sure you show your excitement for a good guess as well as a correct answer.

❸ Then, it's the student's turn to provide the clues and the teacher's turn to guess the object. You may want to make several wild guesses, which may encourage the student to tell you when you are wrong. This process helps you evaluate how well the student understands the concepts involved.

☞ Tip:

Tip: Start simple. You may use just a color as your only attribute at first, and then add a function. You may also limit the choices to items in the classroom or even objects on a table or shelf. Encourage parents to use Guess What while driving in the car or waiting in a line or at the doctor's office with their child.

Idea 25

Count Down

Finding strategies to help students decrease repetitive actions or vocalizations that interfere with learning and socialization can be difficult. One strategy that often works is to provide a variety of cues to the student. Here is a simple visual signal system that can be used in class or on the job by teachers or supervisors, then eventually by students who function independently.

Follow these steps.

❶ Copy the class size numbers 1 through 5 on stiff paper of various colors, and then laminate them for durability. Bind or attach the pages to each other with spiral binding or a metal ring through a punched hole. When you assemble the Count Down sytem, put the 5 card on top, then each number in decreasing order until you get to 1.

❷ Next decide on a time interval and target number of signals (between five and one) you want to use with the student. For frequent, longstanding behaviors, start the countdown with five. For less troublesome or frequent behaviors, start at three. The number of signals you use will depend on the student's age, level of understanding, and typical pattern of behavior. Count the number of times the student engages in the behavior during a specific time period, then set a target level for the behavior slightly lower than that number. Circle your target number on the Count Down Contract.

❸ Decide on a positive reinforcer that the student finds enjoyable or desirable and include the reinforcer in the information on the Count Down Contract.

❹ Then, use a structured teaching model to teach the student that when he or she engages in a problematic repetitive behavior, you will signal by showing him the 5 card. This is the signal to stop. If the student continues, show him or her the 4 card, and so on until you reach the number 1. Teach the student that if there is still a number between 1 and 5 when the timer sounds, he or she will receive a reinforcer. Model these procedures with another student or adult, including a demonstration of someone stopping a repetitive behavior after seeing the number signal. Use reinforcement and verbal praise during the teaching sequence.

❺ Begin the Count Down. Set the timer for the time period you have selected. If the student engages in the targeted repetitive behavior, signal him with a number card. After each signal, show the next number.

❻ When the timer goes off, check the student's cards. If any number between 5 and 1 is remaining, reinforce, praise, smile, cheer, and congratulate. If all the numbers are gone, start the timer again and repeat the sequence.

Note. This idea is adapted from *Project Ride: Responding to Individual Differences in Education*, Elementary School Edition, by R. Beck, 1996, Longmont, CO: Sopris West. Copyright 1996 by Sopris West. Adapted with permission. All rights reserved.

After the student has begun to master the Count Down system with the large cards, introduce the smaller set of personal size cards, which can be put on a key chain or small metal ring. Encourage the student to carry the small set throughout the day. Everyone who interacts with the student should prompt him or her to use the small number cards to self-signal when the words or actions of the student become repetitive. Continue to use frequent enthusiastic praise and some type of tangible or activity reinforcer every time the student has a number card remaining after a work session or class period.

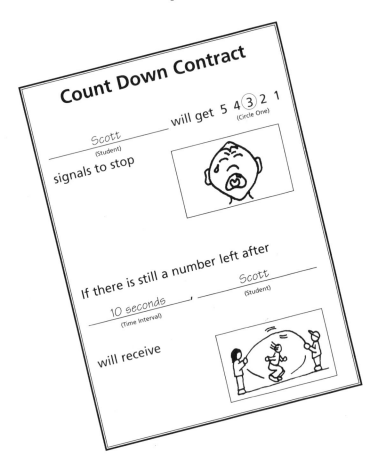

🖝 Tip:

You may decide to use a verbal reminder or warning along with the Count Down system. If so, use your words each time you show the student a number card. Also remember that some students will do better without people talking to them.

Note. The pictures in the example on this page are from *Teaching Kids and Adults With Autism: Building the Framework for Lifetime Learning*, by K. M. Fad and L. R. Moulton, 1999, Longmont, CO: Sopris West. Copyright 1999 by Kathleen McConnell Fad and L. Rozelle Moulton. Reprinted with permission.

Count Down Contract

_____ will get 5 4 3 2 1
(Student)   (Circle One)

signals to stop

If there is still a number left after

_____, _____
(Time Interval)   (Student)

will receive

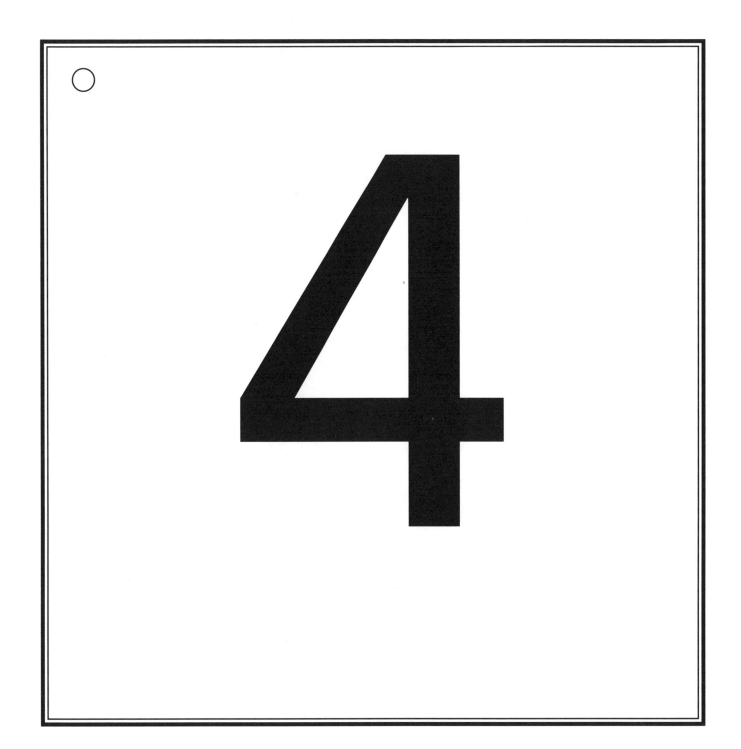

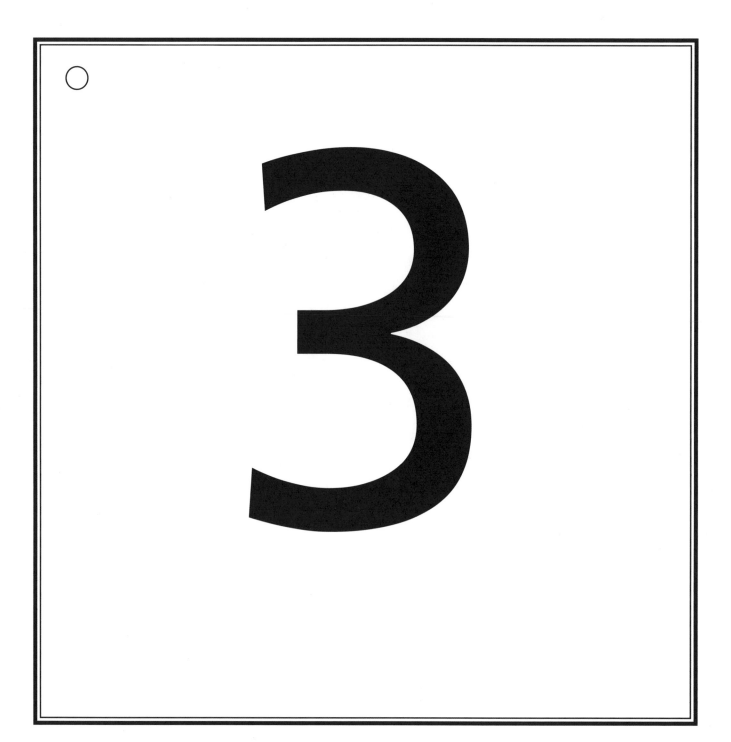

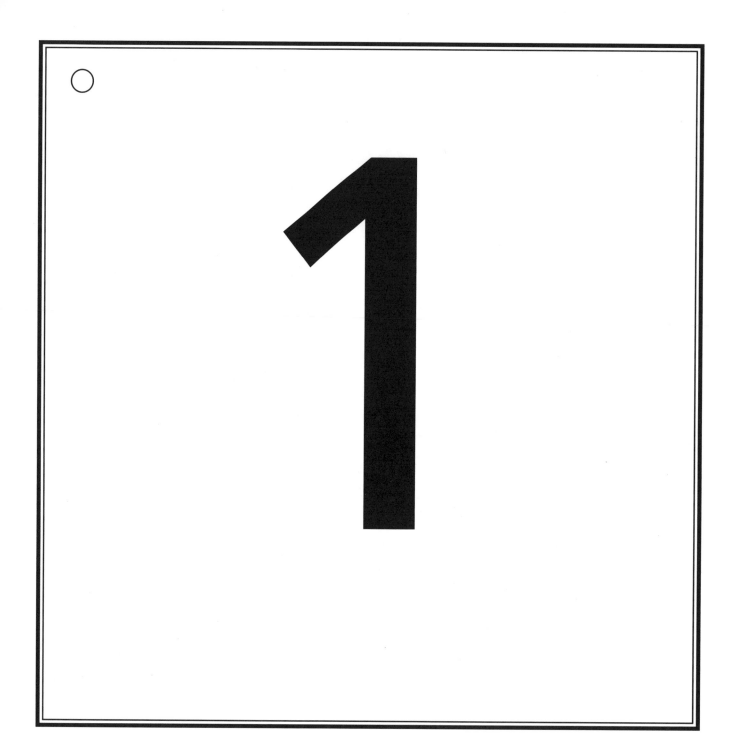

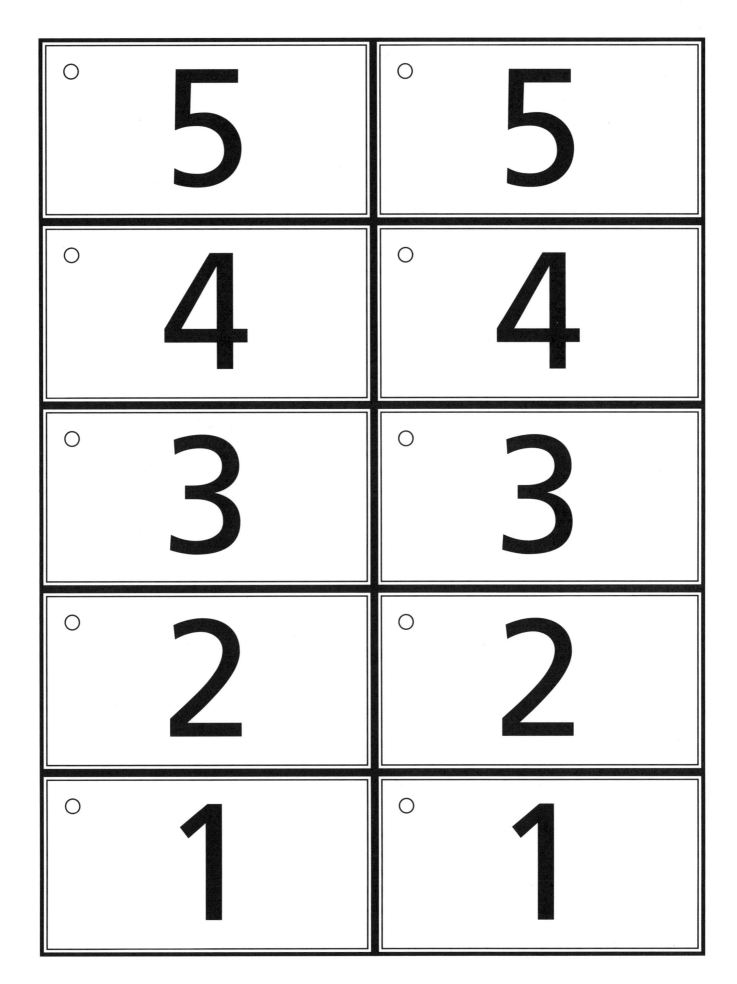

Idea 26
Follow and Find

Sometimes students with autism have problems getting independently from one class or work area to the next. To help students find their way without constantly using verbal reminders or physical guidance, arrange some cues in the environment.

Here are some ideas that work.

❶ Put colored (and laminated) footprints on the floor leading from one place to the next.

❷ When walking in front of the student, shine a small flashlight on the floor behind you.

❸ Put brightly colored arrows at eye level on the hallway walls, so students know which direction to go and when to stop. You may want to put the student's name on the arrows.

❹ Place a door hanger on the doorknob of classrooms that are destinations for students with autism. The door hanger will help students recognize where they are supposed to be.

JORDAN

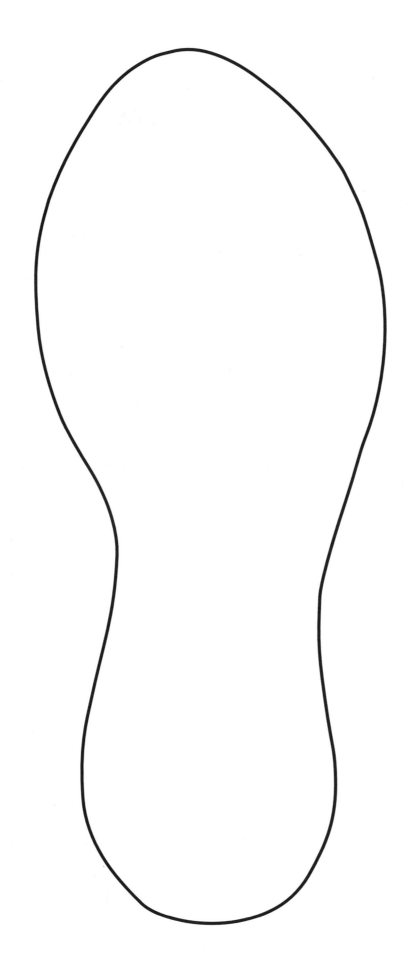

Idea 26

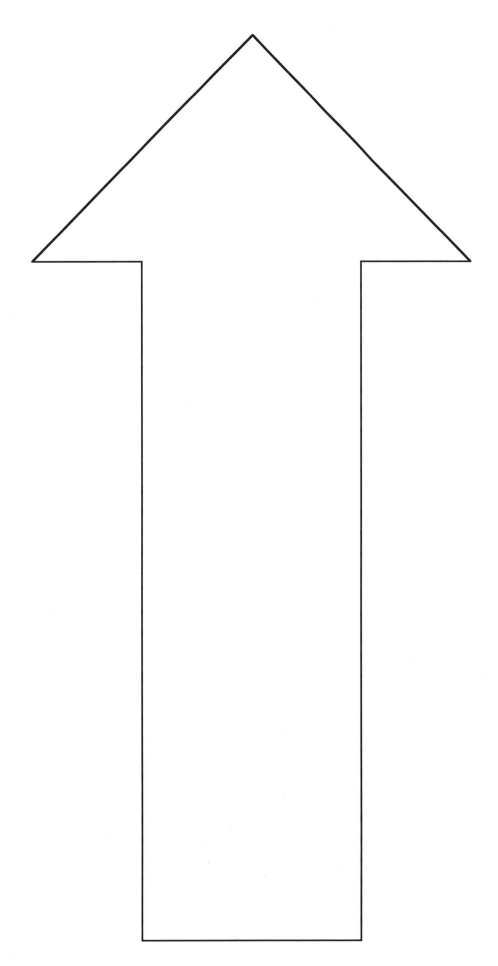

109

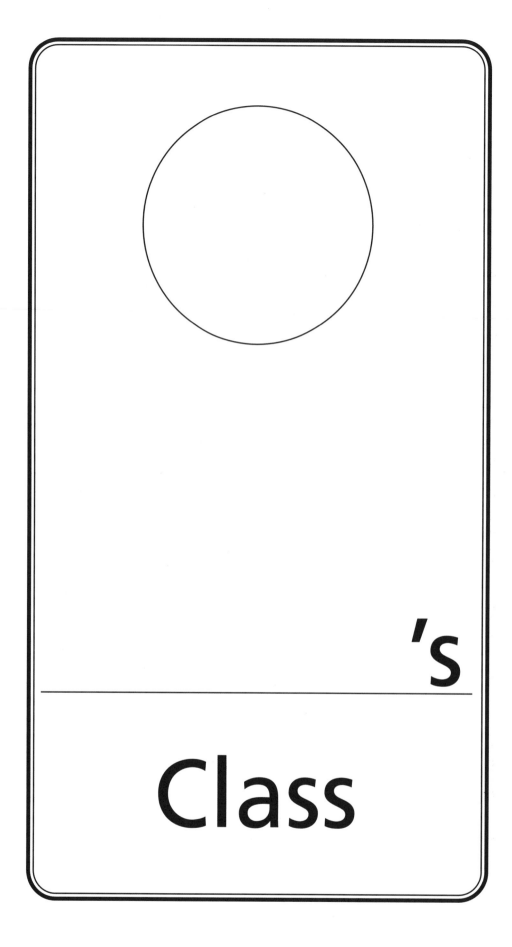

_____'s

Class

Idea 27
Now–Next Picture Map

Students with autism spectrum disorders often have fewer behavior problems when they have consistent, predictable routines in their lives. While the consistency can often prevent problems with changes and transitions, too much consistency and sameness may cause another problem: a lack of flexibility or adaptability. Carried to an extreme, this lack of flexibility can result in ritualistic, repetitive, and unproductive behaviors. In order to provide some predictability in situations but still help students adjust, use simple two-part schedules or picture maps.

The *Now–Next* picture map is a simple tool for helping students transition from one activity to the next. Students should be taught to manage the picture map themselves.

Here's how to use it.

❶ As the student begins an activity, put a picture, symbol, or word on the Now section of the map to indicate what he or she is doing. Attach with fastener loop squares or tacky adhesive.

❷ On the right side, attach a representation of what will happen next. Briefly point to each side and indicate what is happening now and what will happen next.

❸ After completing the task or activity at hand, remove the picture, symbol, or word from the Now side, move the Next picture to the left (so it becomes the Now), and add a new representation of what will happen Next. Once again, tell the student what is happening and then prepare him or her for what will happen next.

Now	Next

Now	Next

Idea 27

Idea 28
Schedule It

If students with autism can learn to follow a daily schedule independently, it will reduce the need for prompting from adults. Following a schedule may also make transitions go more smoothly since students resist change less frequently if they are familiar with their schedules and have a comfortable routine. There are many ways to create and construct schedules.

For students who are nonverbal and/or cannot read, one of the easiest and most convenient resources for constructing a schedule is a set of picture symbol cards (like those from the Mayer-Johnson Company). Select cards that represent the student's daily activities; then arrange them in order with Velcro or by photocopying. You can use any of several different formats, including:

- A photo album or flipbook

- A vertical or horizontal card with symbols attached (See the Daily Schedule forms provided.)

- A list inside a file folder

  For students who can read, schedules should include printed or handwritten words and numbers. As the student completes each activity, he or she can check it or cross it off the schedule.

☞ **Tip:**

If following the schedule for an entire day is too much for a student, begin with one or two activities, then gradually expand.

Order Information for Mayer-Johnson Company

Picture Communication Symbols (PCS). A set of 3200 picture symbols used for communication.

Boardmaker software (Macintosh and Windows). Creates communication displays.

Mayer-Johnson Company
P.O. Box 1579
Solana Beach, CA 92075
Phone 800/588-4548
Fax 858/550-0449
http://www.mayer-johnson.com

Name _____ Date _____

Daily Schedule

Name _____ Date _____

Daily Schedule

1. _____ ☐

2. _____ ☐

3. _____ ☐

4. _____ ☐

5. _____ ☐

6. _____ ☐

7. _____ ☐

Idea 28

Idea 29

Touch, Show, or Find

Although teachers always strive to improve students' expressive language skills, it is also important to increase students' receptive language. When students understand what teachers or family members say, they can follow verbal directions, comprehend instruction, identify objects, demonstrate their understanding of everyday conversations, and participate more actively in the world around them. Even though students with autism may have limited skills in spoken language, good receptive language skills will help the rest of us know whether they understand what we're saying. This will help us keep our expectations high and continue teaching as much as we can.

One strategy for increasing receptive language is to teach students to demonstrate that they know the meanings of commonly used words by touching, showing, or finding objects.

Here are the two components of Touch, Show, or Find.

Decide on the Words to Teach

First, decide on the categories of words you want the student to learn. (These could include family members, people at school, commonly used toys or materials, items of clothing, etc.)

❶ For as many words as possible, locate the actual objects. (The student's favorite toy, an article of clothing, etc.)

❷ Next take photographs or find pictures to represent the words that are too large or unavailable. (Pictures of family members, advertisements with names of restaurants, etc.)

❸ Then arrange the photos, pictures, or objects by categories. Start with the most familiar categories.

Use a Systematic Teaching Model

Once you have your vocabulary words selected, you can begin to teach.

❶ At a table or desk, sit across from or next to the student. Have your first set of photos, pictures, or objects ready to use.

❷ Select the first word you would like to teach (*Mom*, represented by a photograph of the student's mother).

❸ Show the object, picture or photograph to the student. As you do so, touch it, and say the word slowly and clearly ("Mom").

❹ Tell the student to show you the item or touch it. ("Show me *Mom*.") If necessary, guide his hand gently.

❺ As soon as the student touches the item, reinforce him immediately with praise, smiles, cheers, and, if necessary, a tangible reinforcer.

❻ Repeat the procedure at least five to ten times, depending on the age and instructional level of the student.

❼ Next, tell the student to touch the item but this time do not prompt or guide his hand. ("Touch *Mom*" or "Show me *Mom*.")

❽ If he responds by touching the object or photograph, reinforce him immediately. If he does not respond correctly, repeat the teaching sequence.

After the student has mastered a basic set of vocabulary words and can identify them correctly every time, begin to use two objects at a time. This will require the student to discriminate between the two. If he still chooses the correct object, you will be more sure that he really knows the meaning of the word. To encourage even more generalization and to expand your teaching away from the table or desk, begin to give the student a direction to "Find _____" in the classroom, all over the school, in the community, and at home. This will require the student to discriminate among several different objects and enlarge the possibilities for a large and ever-expanding vocabulary.

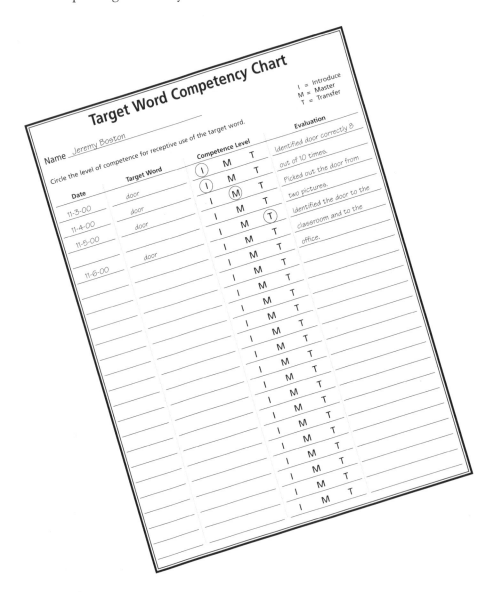

Target Word Competency Chart

I = Introduce
M = Master
T = Transfer

Name: Jeremy Boston

Circle the level of competence for receptive use of the target word.

Date	Target Word	Competence Level			Evaluation
11-3-00	door	(I)	M	T	Identified door correctly 8 out of 10 times.
11-4-00	door	(I)	M	T	Picked out the door from two pictures.
11-5-00	door	I	(M)	T	
		I	M	(T)	Identified the door to the classroom and to the office.
11-6-00	door	I	M	T	
		I	M	T	
		I	M	T	
		I	M	T	
		I	M	T	
		I	M	T	
		I	M	T	
		I	M	T	
		I	M	T	
		I	M	T	
		I	M	T	
		I	M	T	
		I	M	T	
		I	M	T	
		I	M	T	
		I	M	T	
		I	M	T	
		I	M	T	

On the following pages, we provide several materials to help you teach this important skill.

- First you will find a list of commonly used vocabulary words, grouped into categories. This list should help you get started by giving you ideas of what words to teach. Of course, you should start small and keep expanding.

- Next there are some sample vocabulary cards, which are drawings of common vocabulary words you may want to teach students. Of course, you should always use the real object whenever possible, but using photographs or drawings is sometimes necessary. (These particular drawings are from *Teaching Kids and Adults With Autism: Building the Framework for Lifetime Learning* from Sopris West.)

- Because there are many sources of drawings or photographs that can be used to teach receptive language, we have also provided a list of additional resources.

- Finally, you will find a data collection form to use when teaching words. Here's how it works:
  1. Choose a target word or words.
  2. Find cards or everyday objects that depict the target words.
  3. Check the appropriate skill level.
     I = Introduce (*At this level, the child does not consistently demonstrate understanding of the word.*)
     M = Mastery (*At this level, the child demonstrates understanding of the word at a predetermined mastery level. We suggest you use 85%.*)
     T = Transfer (*At this level, the child demonstrates understanding of the word across situations.*)

Note. The nouns, verbs, and emotions/feelings vocabulary cards are from *Teaching Kids and Adults With Autism: Building the Framework for Lifetime Learning*, by K. M. Fad and L. R. Moulton, 1999, Longmont, CO: Sopris West. Copyright 1999 by Kathleen McConnell Fad and L. Rozelle Moulton. Reprinted with permission.

Categories and Words
Receptive Language Instruction

People at Home (teach by name)
Mother/Mom
Father/Dad
Stepparents
Brother(s)
Sister(s)
Grandparents
Extended family members
Family friends
Family pets

People at School (teach by name)
Teachers
Assistants or aides
Principal or director
Classmates
Bus driver
Cafeteria personnel
Speech therapist
Occupational or physical therapist
Volunteers/helpers

Items of Clothing
Pants/slacks
Shorts
Top or shirt
Blouse
Belt
Socks
Shoes
Pajamas/bathrobe
Underpants/shorts
Bra or T-shirt
Bathing suit

Food
The student's favorite foods (teach these first)
Milk
Soft drinks/sodas (by name)
Sandwich
Taco
Hamburger
Pizza
Spaghetti
French fries
Cereal
Bread
Tortilla

Cheese
Chips
Pretzels
Apple
Banana
Pear
Orange
(any others common to the student's home or school)

Toys, Games, Hobbies
Ball
Swing
Bicycle
Puzzle
Car
Truck
Keys
Doll
Drum
Game
TV
VCR
Video
CD or tape

Places
Home
Grandparents' or other relatives' house
Grocery store
Bank
Favorite restaurants (with logo)
Park
Doctor's office
School
Church
Playground

Emergency/Safety Words
Stop
Go
Walk
Boys'/Men's Room
Girls'/Women's Room
Poison
Danger/Dangerous
Caution
In
Out

Other Categories of Words

- Most common words in reading. These lists are especially good for students who have prereading skills. They include the Dolch Words and the Allen List (both contain frequently used sight words).
- Colors
- Numbers (not counting objects, just recognizing the number)
- Animals
- Household objects
- Items of furniture
- Rooms in the home or school
- Adjectives (especially feelings)
- Verbs (especially action verbs)

Vocabulary Cards
Nouns

cat

dog

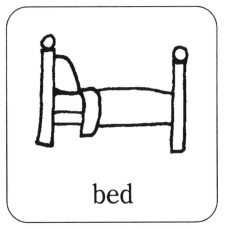

bed

bus

door

library

pants

paper

school

Idea 29

Vocabulary Cards
Verbs

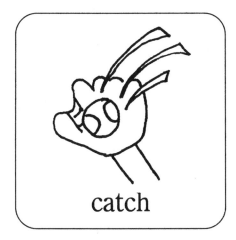
catch

chase

climb

drink

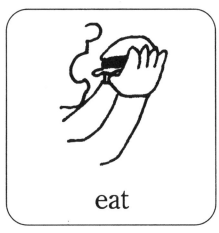
eat

play

run

wash

write

Idea 29

Vocabulary Cards
Emotions/Feelings

cry

angry

excited

frustrated

funny

happy

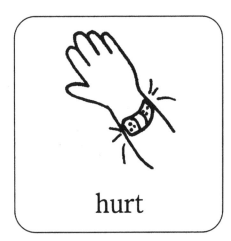

hurt

sad

scared

124

Resources for Picture and Word Cards

The following products are available from PRO-ED.

Comprehensive Receptive and Expressive Vocabulary Test (CREVT)
Photo Picture Book
The picture book is spiral-bound and has 10 full-color picture plates, six pictures per plate. Each plate relates to a theme: animals, transportation, occupations, clothing, food, personal grooming, tools, household appliances, recreation, and clerical materials.

Test of Language Development–Intermediate (TOLD–I:3)
Picture Book
The picture book is spiral-bound and has nine full-color picture plates, six pictures per plate.

Language Making Action Cards
The complete program includes 600 full-color picture cards (480 different picture cards and 120 duplicated cards for matching activities) in a carrying case.

IZIT Cards
The complete program includes four sets of picture and word vocabulary cards (276 cards total) and instructions for playing more than 30 different language games, all in a carrying case.

Silly Sentences
The complete program includes three individually color-coded decks of cards and an instruction booklet in a vinyl storage envelope.

Library of Vocabulary Photographs
The complete program includes 13 picture groups; each group consists of 47 full-color photos of everyday and not-so-everyday items. Each picture group is in a vinyl envelope.

Target Word Competency Chart

Name _____

I = Introduce
M = Master
T = Transfer

Circle the level of competence for receptive use of the target word.

Date	Target Word	Competence Level	Evaluation
		I M T	
		I M T	
		I M T	
		I M T	
		I M T	
		I M T	
		I M T	
		I M T	
		I M T	
		I M T	
		I M T	
		I M T	
		I M T	
		I M T	
		I M T	
		I M T	
		I M T	
		I M T	
		I M T	
		I M T	
		I M T	
		I M T	
		I M T	

Idea 29

Idea 30
Say or Tell Me

Using the materials and teaching model provided in Idea 29, you can begin to build students' expressive language skills. Follow the same procedures for deciding what to teach, gathering materials, and teaching with a systematic model of instruction. This time, however, your objective will be for the student to say the name or tell you the name of the object, person, place, or activity. Your directions (Steps 4 and 5) will be to "Say" or "Tell me."

For example, if you are using the picture of Mom, say the word "Mom" slowly and clearly, point to the photograph, then ask the student to "Say, *Mom*." You may need to prompt or cue the student with beginning sounds "mmmmmm." When the student responds correctly, use lots of enthusiastic praise and positive reinforcement. Record the response on your data recording form.

Once the student can say the names of items correctly, you can encourage higher-level language development by asking him or her to identify objects based on:

❶ Function (Tell me *what you eat with*. That's right, a *spoon*.)

❷ Category (Tell me the *people in your family*. Good, *Mama, Daddy*.)

❸ Form (Tell me something that is *round*. A *ball*. That's right.)

☞ Note:

Some students with autism spectrum disorders are completely nonverbal or have very limited oral language skills. For those students, you may wish to begin expressive language instruction by encouraging production of sounds (See Idea 6, Bring Out the Noise). However, if the student is already saying some words, and you believe he or she has the prerequisite skills to use language in more meaningful and consistent ways, then try this idea. Introduce one word at a time, beginning with those you have already heard the student say.

Target Word Competency Chart

Name _____

Circle the level of competence for expressive use of the target word.

I = Introduce
M = Master
T = Transfer

Date	Target Word	Competence Level	Evaluation
		I M T	
		I M T	
		I M T	
		I M T	
		I M T	
		I M T	
		I M T	
		I M T	
		I M T	
		I M T	
		I M T	
		I M T	
		I M T	
		I M T	
		I M T	
		I M T	
		I M T	
		I M T	
		I M T	
		I M T	
		I M T	
		I M T	
		I M T	
		I M T	

Idea 30

Idea 31
Do This Instead of That

When students with autism are stressed or nervous, they may begin to make repetitive or ritualistic movements and gestures. If the movements involve their hands, face, hair, or eyes, students may become self-injurious. One way to decrease a potentially harmful movement is to teach the student an alternate behavior that is *similar to* but *not as harmful as* his or her typical routine.

Here are some alternative behaviors for students. Ideally, they should be incompatible with the self-injurious behavior (i.e., you can't be doing one if you are doing the other).

Instead of →	Teach the Student to
• hitting chin or face with fist	• squeeze a soft ball
• pulling hair or eyebrows	• hold and rub a fuzzy key chain
• rubbing cheeks or forehead	• rub a worry stone
• slapping thighs	• roll a small, round eraser or sit on hands
• chewing shirt	• wear a collarless shirt and/or chew gum

☞ Remember to:

❶ Think of the alternative, incompatible behavior

❷ Teach it through direct instruction and modeling

❸ Use lots of positive reinforcement to increase student's demonstration of the new behavior

Idea 32
Activity Notebook

To help students decrease the time spent playing with parts of objects, repeatedly twirling or rubbing, or otherwise engaging in repetive, stereotypical movements, try an activity notebook.

Here is how it works.

❶ First find a notebook or folder for the student that he or she can carry from one class or workplace to another.

❷ Next attach adhesive squares to the inside cover of the notebook. These will be used to manage small, functional items.

❸ Also insert a clear plastic zippered pouch or case into the front of the notebook. (You can buy these already made with a three-hole edge or tab so they fit into notebooks.)

❹ Then choose some items for the student that are age appropriate and situation appropriate. (You may need to brainstorm with parents and other professionals.)

❺ Finally, insert the items that are available to the student, allowing him or her to choose an activity. Focus on objects, photos, and activities that are typical for his or her age group and situation. Small items go on the front cover, larger items in the pouch.

❻ Change the items periodically so that the student doesn't become stereotypical with this new set of objects.

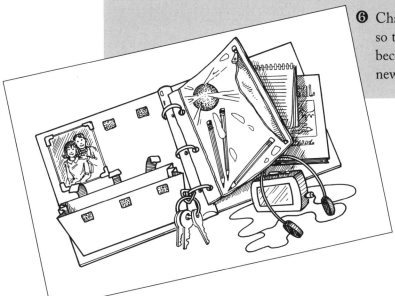

☞ **Tip:**

Following are things you may want to include in the notebook:

- Photos of family and friends
- Playing cards
- A calculator
- A small notepad with pencil or pen
- A small, short book if the student reads
- Magazines or comic books
- Crossword or dot-to-dot puzzles
- Earphones with a CD player or tape player
- Squeeze balls of soft material
- Keys on a keychain (don't put the essential keys here, only old ones)
- Miniature writing slates that erase by lifting a page

Idea 33

Less Time → Choice Time

Stereotypical behaviors can make students seem odd or different from their peers and may prevent them from getting involved with others. Here's a practical way to reduce the time a student with autism spends engaged in a repetitive or stereotypical behavior:

❶ Decide on the exact behavior you think the student should do less often (i.e., the target behavior). Write it on the Less Time → Choice Time Record/Goal Form.

❷ Time the target behavior during the same interval (10 minutes, 30 minutes, one class period, etc.) every day for a week. Record the daily time and the weekly average on the Less Time → Choice Time Record/Goal Form. To make the timing accurate, wear a stopwatch around your neck. Every time the student starts the target behavior, click the stopwatch on. When he or she stops the behavior, click the stopwatch off but *do not reset the stopwatch.* At the end of the interval, you'll have a total amount of time the student has spent engaging in the stereotypical behavior. Record the total for each day as well as the average for the week and graph the weekly average on the graph provided.

❸ Set a goal to reduce the amount of time the student spends on the targeted behavior. Explain the goal, using language and a level of detail appropriate to the student's age and level of understanding. You may want to begin with a reduction of 10% to 20%. Record your goal on the form and if the student is able, have him or her mark a line on the graph representing the goal. Explain that if the student meets the goal, he or she will have "choice time" to choose a favorite activity.

❹ Decide what verbal reinforcement to use, and begin to reinforce the student with enthusiastic praise every time he or she is doing *something other than* the stereotypical target behavior—anything! To remind yourself to reinforce, either make slashes on a small piece of paper or use a timer. Be sure to reinforce very often, possibly 10 times per hour at first. Also consider how much choice time the student can earn and what his or her menu of choices might be.

❺ While you are reinforcing, continue to record the amount of time the student spends engaged in the target behavior. At the end of each day, record and graph the amount, then compute the daily average at the end of each week. Review the student's progress with him or her and see if the goal has been met. If so, the student earns "choice time," an interval during which the student can choose an enjoyable activity (one less stereotypical). You can use the Less Time → Choice Time Menu to help the student understand the process. You can decide on the amount of choice time before you begin the process or tie it directly to reductions in the target behavior (e.g., allow 2 minutes of choice time for each minute he reduces the target behavior). Your approach should be based on the student's functioning level.

❻ When the goal is reached, celebrate, review your plan, and set a new goal!

☞ Tip:

You may need to use some tangible reinforcement along with the verbal praise, especially if the student is very young or has been engaging in the target behavior for a long time. This strategy would work very well with tokens that can be traded in for "choice time." We have provided some clock tokens you may wish to use.

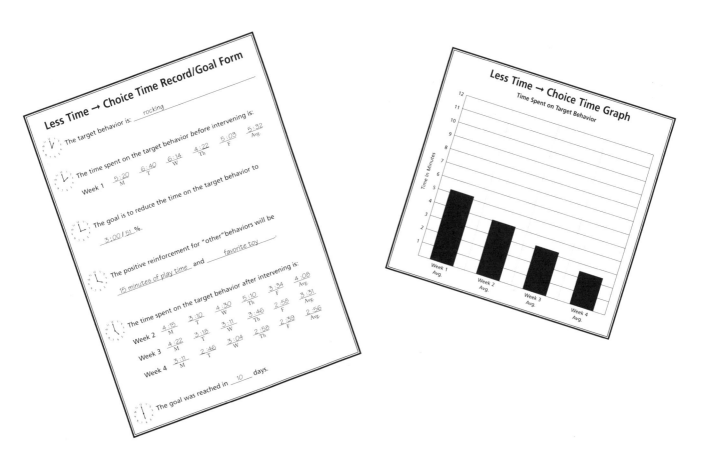

Less Time → Choice Time Record/Goal Form

 The target behavior is _____

 The time spent on the target behavior *before* intervening is:

Week 1 $\dfrac{\quad:\quad}{M}$ $\dfrac{\quad:\quad}{T}$ $\dfrac{\quad:\quad}{W}$ $\dfrac{\quad:\quad}{Th}$ $\dfrac{\quad:\quad}{F}$ $\dfrac{\quad:\quad}{Avg.}$

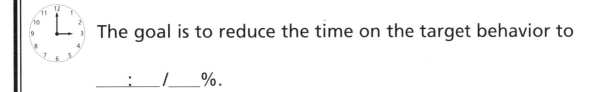

The goal is to reduce the time on the target behavior to

____:____ / ____%.

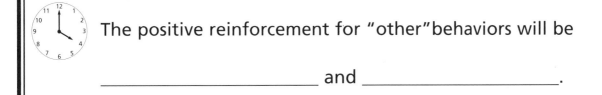

The positive reinforcement for "other" behaviors will be

_____ and _____.

The time spent on the target behavior after intervening is:

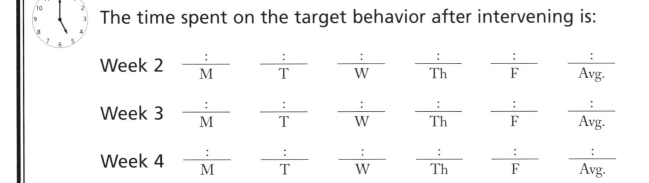

Week 2 $\dfrac{\quad:\quad}{M}$ $\dfrac{\quad:\quad}{T}$ $\dfrac{\quad:\quad}{W}$ $\dfrac{\quad:\quad}{Th}$ $\dfrac{\quad:\quad}{F}$ $\dfrac{\quad:\quad}{Avg.}$

Week 3 $\dfrac{\quad:\quad}{M}$ $\dfrac{\quad:\quad}{T}$ $\dfrac{\quad:\quad}{W}$ $\dfrac{\quad:\quad}{Th}$ $\dfrac{\quad:\quad}{F}$ $\dfrac{\quad:\quad}{Avg.}$

Week 4 $\dfrac{\quad:\quad}{M}$ $\dfrac{\quad:\quad}{T}$ $\dfrac{\quad:\quad}{W}$ $\dfrac{\quad:\quad}{Th}$ $\dfrac{\quad:\quad}{F}$ $\dfrac{\quad:\quad}{Avg.}$

 The goal was reached in _____ days.

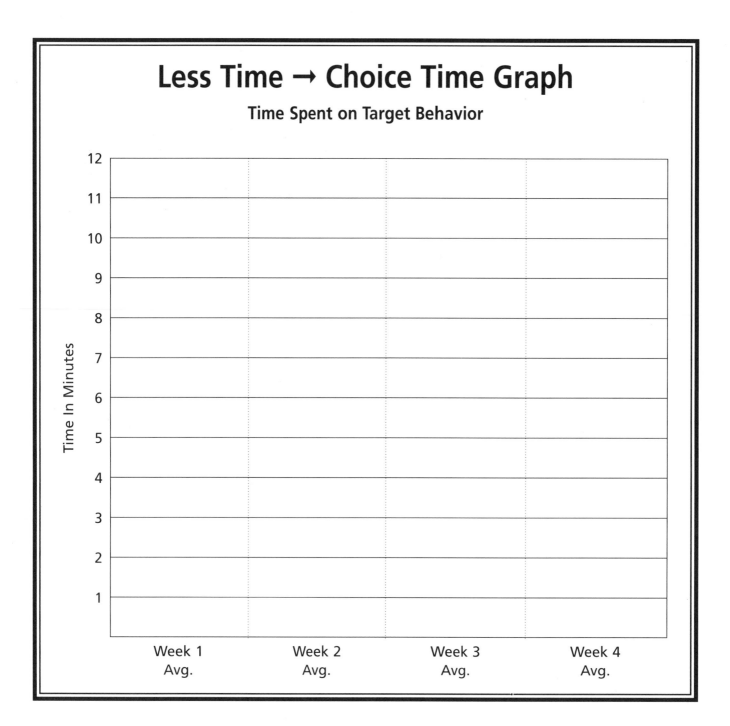

Less Time → Choice Time Graph

Time Spent on Target Behavior

Time In Minutes			
12			
11			
10			
9			
8			
7			
6			
5			
4			
3			
2			
1			
Week 1 Avg.	Week 2 Avg.	Week 3 Avg.	Week 4 Avg.

Idea 33

Less Time → Choice Time Tokens

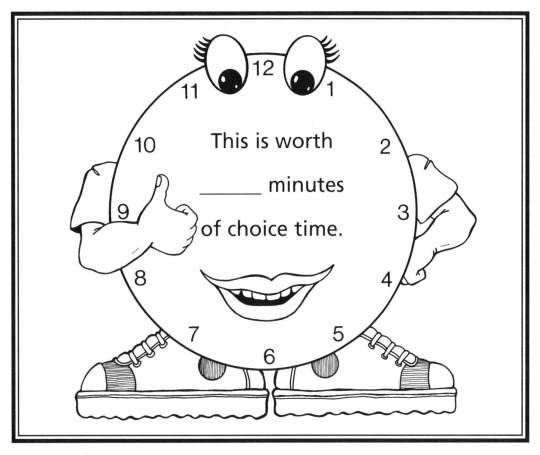

This is worth _____ minutes of choice time.

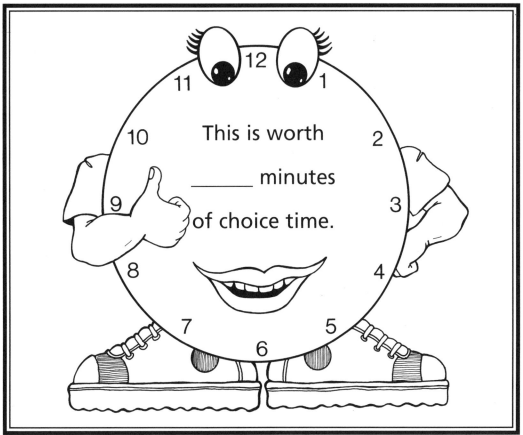

This is worth _____ minutes of choice time.

Idea 33

Less Time → Choice Time Menu

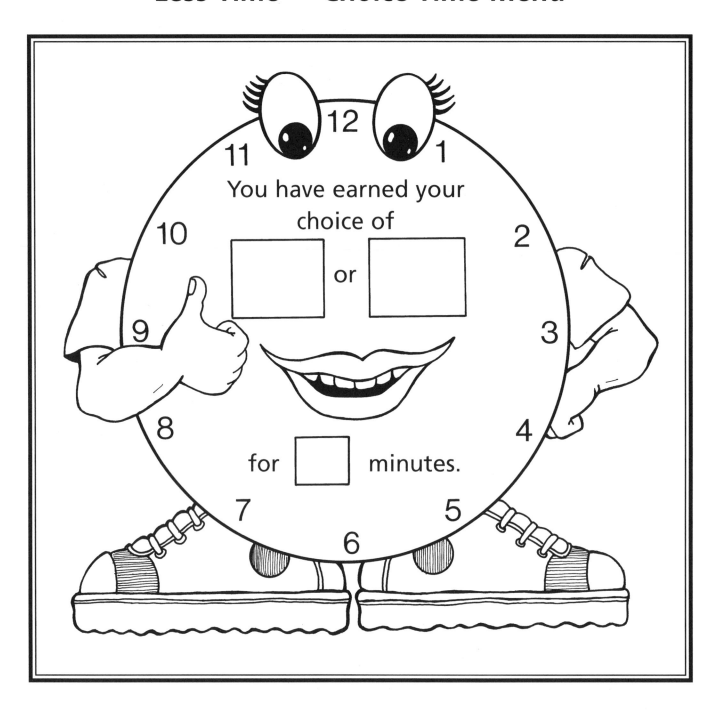

You have earned your choice of

☐ or ☐

for ☐ minutes.

Indicate choices and time with written or visual information.

Idea 33

Idea 34
Nickels, Dimes, or Quarters

Many students with autism understand the value of money. When they do, coins can be used as part of a positive reinforcement system for specific target behviors. Here's a quick and easy system for students who are interested in earning money.

❶ First select a target behavior to increase. Choose something that is observable and easy to measure or count (e.g., saying "hello").

❷ Next decide how frequently you will reinforce the student and determine your criterion (the student should say "hello" when greeted by someone else and will be given the opportunity once every 15 minutes).

❸ Using a coin tube, reinforce the student with a coin each time he or she says "hello" to someone who has said it to him or her. Put the coins in the tube, and along with the coin, give the student lots of praise and enthusiastic smiles.

❹ At the end of the day, empty the coins into the student's wallet or a clear plastic bag and send them home. Parents or caregivers can let the student spend the money on the weekend.

☞ Tip:

We usually ask parents to provide the coins and "recycle" them from home to school.

Idea 35
Card Counters

When teaching new behaviors to students with an autism spectrum disorder, it is often a good idea to use a system of positive reinforcement that is concrete, visual, and easy to manage. Card Counters are a great way to ensure all three of these characteristics. The four samples provided here can be used to record and reinforce students each time they demonstrate a target behavior. The Card Counters included here are the following:

- punch cards
- color cards
- sticker cards
- dot-to-dot cards

Set a goal with the student; then, after each occurrence of the target behavior, punch with a hole punch, color in with a marker, cover the holes with small stickers, or make a line. Students enjoy seeing their progress, and you have a simple management and reinforcement system.

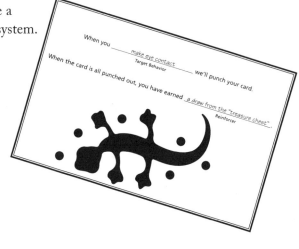

Note. The Card Counters on the following three pages are adapted from *Practical Ideas That Really Work for Students with ADHD*, by K. McConnell, G. Ryser, and J. Higgins, 1999, Austin, TX: PRO-ED, Inc. Copyright 1999 by PRO-ED, Inc. Adapted with permission.

When you _____ we'll punch your card.
Target Behavior

When the card is all punched out, you have earned _____.
Reinforcer

When you _____ we'll punch your card.
Target Behavior

When the card is all punched out, you have earned _____.
Reinforcer

Idea 35

When you _____ we'll color your card.

Target Behavior

When the card is all colored, you have earned _____.

Reinforcer

When you _____ we'll color your card.

Target Behavior

When the card is all colored, you have earned _____.

Reinforcer

Idea 35

When you _____ we'll put a sticker on your card.
Target Behavior

When all of the dots are covered, you have earned _____.
Reinforcer

When you _____ we'll put a sticker on your card.
Target Behavior

When all of the dots are covered, you have earned _____.
Reinforcer

Idea 35

When you _____ we'll draw a line on your card.
                        Target Behavior

When all of the lines are drawn, you have earned _____.
                                                              Reinforcer

20   21
19   1

18
17   15

16   2

                              4
                                5
                          3
                              6

                            10
14   11

                    7

13   12   9   8

Idea 35

When you _____ we'll draw a line on your card.

Target Behavior

When all of the lines are drawn, you have earned _____.

Reinforcer

1   6

2   5

3   4

Idea 36
Use What Works: Positive Reinforcement

Since we know that using positive reinforcement is a great way to increase students' use of skills, we're always looking for ways to use reinforcement effectively. For young students or students who need a very basic, concrete system of reinforcement, consider these options:

❶ Each time the student demonstrates a behavior you have taught and encouraged, add a bright neon ping-pong ball to a plastic jar or other clear container. When the jar is full, the student has earned a privilege or other reinforcer.

❷ Create a paper chain with strips of paper that you staple around each other to form links. Add a link each time you see the target behavior.

❸ Use the paper chain idea, except use the student's own handprints. You can either trace them on paper or make prints using finger paint and cut them out.

❹ Put a flag or balloon at ground level against a wall or doorway. Each time the student demonstrates the behavior, raise the flag or balloon a little bit. When it reaches the ceiling, the student has earned his or her positive reinforcement.

In addition to these concrete ideas, it is always a good idea to start using very basic monitoring systems with students who can understand them. It is important that the daily point sheet or report form be age appropriate and clear. Select from a menu of reinforcers ahead of time and vary the reinforcers often so that students do not become saturated with any one item or activity.

We have provided two positive behavior contracts. The first form is designed for use with young students or those just beginning to focus on targeted behavior goals. The second positive behavior contract is divided into class periods. It is appropriate for older, more independent students. Choose specific target behaviors and then fill in the form with picture symbols, photographs, or words. Use the contract throughout the day to monitor and reinforce student's behaviors.

Here's a list of ideas for reinforcers.

Line leader	Water the plants
Messenger	A good note to take home
Music director (choose music to listen to)	Ice cream
Computer time	Soft drink
Take a walk	Pretzels/chips
Puzzle/game time	Art supplies
Time to draw, color, or other art activity	Bookmarks
Lunch with your favorite teacher	Stickers
Extra break time	A story read aloud by the teacher
Grab something from the grab bag	Popcorn and video party

☞ Tip:

Laminate the contracts so that they can be wiped off and reused.

Directions for Using the Positive Behavioral Contracts

The First Form

❶ Choose two basic target behaviors and two reinforcers. Indicate the goals to students by using pictures or symbols that represent the behaviors and reinforcers selected. (Our example has sitting and no hitting as the target behaviors; cookie and listen to music are the reinforcers.)

❷ Fill in the time intervals, circle the faces, and reinforce if the behavior has been on target.

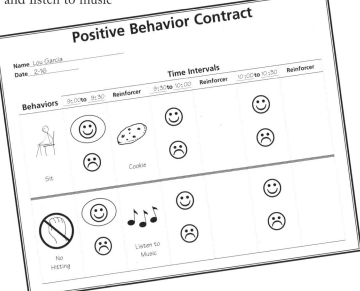

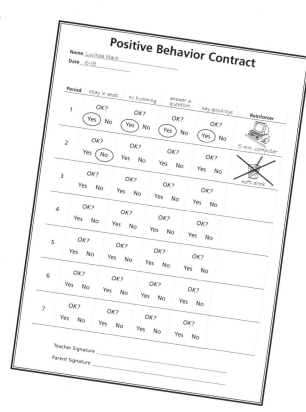

The Second Form

❶ Select four key target behaviors. Indicate them in the boxes across the top of the form.

❷ In the right column, indicate the reinforcers selected by the student.

❸ Circle *Yes* if the behavior is appropriate, and *No* if not. If a target behavior is not met during a period, cross off the reinforcer for that period and move on to the next.

149

Positive Behavior Contract

Name _____

Date _____

Time Intervals

Behaviors	_:_ to _:_	Reinforcer	_:_ to _:_	Reinforcer	_:_ to _:_	Reinforcer
	🙂 🙁		🙂 🙁		🙂 🙁	
	🙂 🙁		🙂 🙁		🙂 🙁	

Idea 36

Positive Behavior Contract

Name_____

Date_____

Period					Reinforcer
1	OK? Yes No	OK? Yes No	OK? Yes No	OK? Yes No	
2	OK? Yes No	OK? Yes No	OK? Yes No	OK? Yes No	
3	OK? Yes No	OK? Yes No	OK? Yes No	OK? Yes No	
4	OK? Yes No	OK? Yes No	OK? Yes No	OK? Yes No	
5	OK? Yes No	OK? Yes No	OK? Yes No	OK? Yes No	
6	OK? Yes No	OK? Yes No	OK? Yes No	OK? Yes No	
7	OK? Yes No	OK? Yes No	OK? Yes No	OK? Yes No	

Teacher Signature _____

Parent Signature _____

Idea 36

Idea 37
Watch and Learn

Before developing a behavioral intervention plan for a student with an autism spectrum disorder, it is important to closely observe the student before, during, and after the behavior. This observation should be used as the basis for analyzing the behavior to determine why it is occurring and what the purpose of the behavior might be. Once this analysis is completed, it should be easier to design an effective intervention plan. The Watch and Learn form is a simple and easy way to record your observations. It is structured to help you focus on each important component of the student's pattern of behavior.

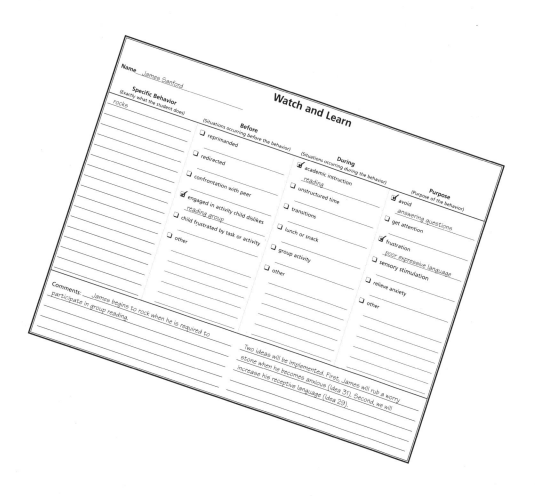

Watch and Learn

Name _____

Specific Behavior (Exactly what the student does)	Before (Situations occurring *before* the behavior)	During (Situations occurring *during* the behavior)	Purpose (Purpose of the behavior)
	☐ reprimanded	☐ academic instruction	☐ avoid
	☐ redirected	☐ unstructured time	☐ get attention
	☐ confrontation with peer	☐ transitions	☐ frustration
	☐ engaged in activity child dislikes	☐ lunch or snack	☐ sensory stimulation
	☐ child frustrated by task or activity	☐ group activity	☐ relieve anxiety
	☐ other	☐ other	☐ other

Comments: _____

Idea 37